Bosnia's Million Bones

Bosnia's Million Bones

SOLVING THE WORLD'S GREATEST FORENSIC PUZZLE

CHRISTIAN JENNINGS

palgrave

macmillan

BOSNIA'S MILLION BONES

Copyright © Christian Jennings, 2013.

All rights reserved.

First published in 2013 by
PALGRAVE MACMILLAN®
in the U.S.—a division of St. Martin's Press LLC,
175 Fifth Avenue, New York, NY 10010.

Where this book is distributed in the UK, Europe and the rest of the world,
this is by Palgrave Macmillan, a division of Macmillan Publishers Limited,
registered in England, company number 785998, of Houndmills,
Basingstoke, Hampshire RG21 6XS.

Palgrave Macmillan is the global academic imprint of the above companies
and has companies and representatives throughout the world.

Palgrave® and Macmillan® are registered trademarks in the United States,
the United Kingdom, Europe and other countries.

ISBN: 978–1–137–27868–5

The Library of Congress has catalogued the hardcover edition as follows:

Jennings, Christian.
    Bosnia's million bones : solving the world's greatest forensic puzzle /
  by Christian Jennings.
       pages cm
    1. Criminal investigation—Bosnia and Hercegovina. 2. Forensic
  sciences—Bosnia and Hercegovina. 3. Genocide—Bosnia and
  Hercegovina. I. Title.

HV8073.J456 2013
364.15_10949742—dc23   2013014615

A catalogue record of the book is available from the British Library.

Design by Newgen Knowledge Works (P) Ltd., Chennai, India.

First edition: November 2013

10 9 8 7 6 5 4 3 2 1

Printed in the United States of America.

For my mother, Mariella Jennings, and late father,
Michael Jennings, Military Cross

Contents

Acknowledgments

My thanks go to the following people, for all sorts of help, advice, humor, and ideas, not just during the writing of this book but also during seven years living and working in Sarajevo: Kurt Bassuener, Nerma Jelačić, Jasmin Agović, Jasmina Mameledžija, Valery Perry, Esma Aličehajić, James Fenn, Chris Parker, Aida Čerkez, Neil MacDonald, Beth Kampschror, Zinaida Ilaria, Anisa Sućeska-Vekić, Tara Zapp, and Robert Wolf.

And of course, thanks, gratitude, and much else go, without exception, to Zahida Drače.

Andrew Lownie did an exceptional job with his literary agenting skills, and thanks to Luba Ostashevsky, not just as an astute and excellent editor, but also as the person who, of everybody, best saw and executed the idea behind this book.

I'm very grateful to all at the International Commission on Missing Persons, most particularly Kathryne Bomberger, Adam Boys, Tom Parsons, Ian Hanson, Andreas Kleiser, Edin Jašaragić, and Adi Rizvić. And to all those elsewhere who gave assistance and contributed in many different ways to this book, but who shall remain anonymous.

Eighteen years after the Bosnian war, some buildings in Sarajevo are still bullet-scarred ruins. Adam Boys, the ICMP's Chief Operating Officer, stands near one, opposite Sarajevo's zoo. Copyright Jasmin Agović Photography.

Kathryne Bomberger, the Director-General of ICMP. Following her determination to help account for the thousands of persons missing from Srebrenica, Bosnia, and the Balkans conflicts, the organization became a global leader in dealing with missing persons. Copyright the ICMP.

Kada Hotic, the Vice-President of the Association of Mothers of Srebrenica and Zepa Enclaves, holds a photograph of her husband and children. Her son and husband were both killed around Srebrenica in 1995. Her daughter now lives near Sarajevo. Sarajevo, 2013. Copyright Jasmin Agović Photography.

The mortuary at the Podrinje Identification Project in Tuzla, north-eastern Bosnia, where thousands of human remains of Srebrenica victims are stored awaiting identification and burial. Copyright Jasmin Agović Photography.

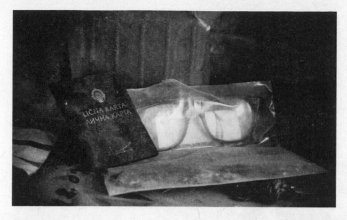

Along with corpses and body parts, thousands of different artifacts were also found in mass graves in Bosnia. Here a clock and an identity card stand with other victims' possessions exhumed along with their remains. Copyright Jasmin Agović Photography.

A Bosnian osteologist from the ICMP examines a human tooth to enable her to estimate the age of the owner at time of death. Copyright Jasmin Agović Photography.

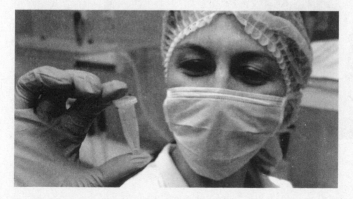

A laboratory technician from the ICMP shows a liquid sample containing human DNA. Copyright Jasmin Agović Photography

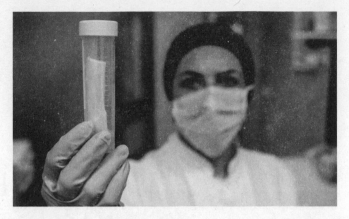

A human bone sample is shown prepared for treatment prior to entering the ICMP's identification system. Copyright Jasmin Agović Photography.

At the Lukavac Reassociation Centre in north-eastern Bosnia, the different co-mingled body-parts of Srebrenica victims exhumed from mass graves are painstakingly pieced together before being returned to the victims' relatives. Copyright Jasmin Agović Photography.

The Agricultural Cooperative warehouses at Kravica, some six miles from Srebrenica, were the scene of mass executions where over 1,000 men were estimated to have been machine gunned in July 1995. Bullet-scarred and dark, they stand there today. Copyright Jasmin Agović Photography.

Chapter One

HOW DOES A COUNTRY RECOVER AFTER A GENOCIDE?

SARAJEVO, SUMMER 2012

It is a hot Saturday morning in June on Kulovica Street in central Sarajevo—93 degrees of scorching, dry summer heat in the Bosnian capital. The Hotel Bosnia sits in the middle of the thoroughfare, and the pitted, gray tarmac of the surrounding streets still bears the unmistakable fragmentation marks of mortar strikes—a by-product of the four-year-long siege of the city that ended in 1995.

However, life is moving on in Bosnia. Today it remains a land of haves and have-nots, but there are signs of progress. For some—those with money, political power, influence, jobs, initiative, and confidence—things are moving slowly forward. Many of the buildings around the hotel, like hundreds across Bosnia and the former Yugoslavia, bear splashes of new plaster covering the wartime bullet scars. Kulovica Street leads down toward the Čobanija Bridge, which crosses Sarajevo's narrow River Miljacka. From its banks, Bosnian fishermen float maggots and flecks of cheese down the current of the gin-clear waters, hoping to tempt the small *klen* that flicker through the shallows.[1] Mountains appear above the river. The city is surrounded by hills, one reason why it was so easy for the Bosnian Serb forces to besiege it during the war.

But on this particular summer day, with the war long over, the hotel serves as a venue for hosting the twenty-first International Meeting on Forensic Medicine, organized by the medical faculty of Sarajevo University.[2] A team of Albanian scientists presents a workshop on "Autopsy Findings in the Putrefaction Process," while forensic experts from Italy use detailed and graphic slides for their talk, which they call "An Unusual Case of Suicide with an Electric Saw." Bosnians present their latest findings on determining age at time of death by examining the translucency of the root of the human tooth, and two Germans talk the audience through "The Discovery and Identification of a Corpse Left in a Lake for Ten Years." Italians make a second presentation, called "Double Murder by Crossbow Arrows—From Crime Scene Investigation to Autopsy." Some Macedonians tell delegates about "Occurrence of Acute Subdural Hematoma and Diffuse Axonal Injury as Two Typical Acceleration-related Injuries." The topics range from those with broad implications for the international community to those narrowly focused on aberrant circumstances. (None seems more specialized than a Hungarian forensic team's talk entitled "Fatal Injury Caused by Domestic Swine Tusk.") Regardless, at the Hotel Bosnia, forensic science is the order of the day—and the most logical place in the world for such a gathering of specialists.

Bosnia, although at peace, is still struggling in many ways—politically, socially, psychologically, and economically—to come to terms with the events that took place from 1992 to 1995, and the forensic conference in the hotel is an example of how Bosnian society is attempting to understand and reconcile its gruesome past with its peaceful present. In a conference room, an American forensic scientist from Ohio, working for the Sarajevo-based International Commission on Missing Persons (ICMP), displays a complicated graphic on a large white screen that shows interlocking lines and semicircles colored in purple, green, orange, pink, and blue. The scientist explains the links between five primary execution sites where several thousand Bosnian Muslim men were machine-gunned outside the town of Srebrenica in eastern Bosnia in 1995, the only incidence of genocide to have taken place in Europe since the Holocaust, and the largest massacre of the Bosnian war.[3] The American shows some of the primary mass grave sites where the victims were initially buried, such as Branjevo Farm, Kravica Warehouse, Kozluk, Petkovici Dam, and Lazete. He says that forensic experts have so far been able to gather DNA from some 13,000 bone samples from these sites, which have yielded over 5,500 unique DNA profiles, allowing the scientists to link all of the different execution sites and mass graves together.

*   *   *

The burial sites on the map are centered around three small villages and towns in eastern Bosnia, marked Srebrenica, Potočari, and Bratunac. By 1995, toward the end of the war, more than 50,000 Bosnian Muslim civilians displaced from surrounding areas by three years of fighting had poured into Srebrenica, where they were protected by an ad hoc force of irregular Bosnian Muslim fighters and soldiers from the Army of Bosnia and Herzegovina. Opposing forces from the Bosnian Serb Army surrounded them. A battalion of Dutch United Nations peacekeepers was stationed there too, and the UN mission mandated to operate in Bosnia in that fourth year of the war had declared the enclave a "safe haven." Srebrenica's occupants did not expect to be attacked by the Bosnian Serb forces, and if they were, they fully expected the Dutch soldiers to protect them and NATO to deploy airstrikes from its bases on the eastern seaboard of Italy and from the American Navy carrier battle groups stationed on the Adriatic.

They would be very disappointed on both counts.

Bosnian Serb forces stormed the enclave on July 11, 1995, and thousands of the male occupants were captured as they tried to flee. The number of persons subsequently reported missing to national and international organizations was more than 7,500 men.[4] Soldiers executed most of them and buried them in nearby mass graves.[5] In August 1995, the US ambassador to the UN, Madeleine Albright, stood up in front of a closed session of the UN Security Council to display US Air Force aerial photographs showing hundreds of the captured Srebrenica men sitting on the football field in the small farming village of Nova Kasaba, a few miles from Srebrenica. Two days later, photographs taken from the sky showed the men were gone.[6]

Realizing the judicial net was closing in on them as the war was ending in autumn 1995, the Bosnian Serbs made a bold and enormous attempt to hide the evidence. They dug up the remains of the thousands of executed men and buried their decomposing bodies and body parts in dozens of secondary mass graves in a twenty-mile radius of Srebrenica, over some 300 square miles of countryside. In woods and valleys, along minor roads and on farmlands the human remains broken up by the bulldozers' blades and mechanical diggers' clawed shovels were intermingled—a head here, part of a torso here—and the whole appalling human residue of Srebrenica was reburied. Years later, parts of one man's body were found in four different mass graves miles apart.[7]

But while the Serb perpetrators were hastily digging up the original mass graves and moving the contents, they were leaving a trail. Excavating and moving thousands of decomposing bodies takes manpower and machinery. And the Bosnian Serb Army officers were good Yugoslav bureaucrats, raised in the ordered, quasi-Communist regime of Marshal Josip Broz Tito, who had governed for forty years after World War II, before Yugoslavia broke up. The army logged each mechanical digger, lorry, and bulldozer, along with the petrol and rations. The signatures that were scrawled hurriedly over military petrol requisitions, as growling lorries hauled hundreds of putrescent, decomposing corpses across the narrow back roads of eastern Bosnia, would one day come back to haunt them.

Also, soil mineralogy provided clues. Scientists identified distinctive dirt and rocks carried on, and with, bodies that were moved from execution site to primary burial pit to secondary mass grave. Different ligatures used to tie prisoners' hands before execution provided further specificity, as did such seemingly arcane details like the wheat pollen from one execution site in a cornfield that was subsequently found in a soil analysis from a mass grave. Bodies executed near a bottling plant were found in graves miles away with shards of green glass stuck in their bodies and clothing; soil moved with victims machine-gunned near a dam containing the "tailings" of red mud from a bauxite mining plant was found miles away in the form of water-diluted red mineral dust from the mine.

There was a story to be told, an irrefutable account of atrocities that simply required putting all these puzzle pieces together. Except that there was nothing simple about it.

*   *   *

Before the war began in 1992, Bosnia was a quiet, sedate, and beautiful backwater, one of the six republics that made up Marshal Tito's Socialist Federal Republic of Yugoslavia, lying tucked away across the blue Adriatic Sea from Italy. In the west it borders Italy and Austria, in the north Hungary and Romania, and in the east Bulgaria, Greece, and Albania. To the south is the Adriatic Sea. The seventh son of a Croat father and Slovene mother, Tito was the youngest sergeant-major ever in the Austro-Hungarian army. He was wounded and captured by the Russians in World War I, imprisoned in a Urals work camp that he escaped twice, recaptured, and ultimately set free around 1917, the year of the October Revolution. He had seen more than his fill of the

harsh downside of communism. In World War II he was the leader of
the Yugoslav partisans who fought against the Germans and their ultra-
nationalist Croatian allies. He was a war hero, and a huge variety of foreign governments awarded him a total of 98 decorations for his service.
After the war he led the Non-Aligned Movement, rejecting the Soviet-
style state authoritarianism that he saw to the east in favor of a national
form of communism. And he kept NATO at bay to the west, too. He
brought the constituent republics of Yugoslavia together under the banner of "Brotherhood and Unity," cleverly suppressing internal ethnic
divides, ensuring economic stability, and keeping the snapping jaws of
the myriad of Cold War wolves away from his country's door. Tito was a
bullish, avuncular dictator who understood his people and saw that the
best way to keep the country's ethnic Serbs, Croats, and Muslims from
cutting each other's throats was to bring them together under a gentle
banner of communism-lite. Everybody did national service in the army,
political dissent was quashed, and under a cult of personality, Tito governed absolutely. But then, in May 1980, he died.

In Bosnia, relatively little happened. The countryside was beautiful.
A regional production boom and international borrowing kept the economy in the post-war world. There were jobs for all, and the state employ-
ment structure ensured housing, holidays, and healthcare. Peace prevailed.
Nobody thought war would come again. Years later, many Bosnians were
to wax nostalgic and look back on this period as a kind of halcyon era: no
more so than the months surrounding the 1984 Winter Olympic Games,
held in and around Sarajevo, when the world's focus was on the mountains
around the city, on sport, the great leveler, and on Sarajevo's rather individual people. Even though Tito had been dead for four years, it was as though
his mantra of togetherness still burned bright.

Across the River Drina, by the end of the 1980s, the Serbian
president Slobodan Milošević had other ideas. In their indictment against
Milošević, The Hague Tribunal—the International Criminal Tribunal

for the former Yugoslavia (ICTY)—claimed that Milošević's agenda was one of Serbian nationalism. The latter had been firmly banned under Tito, as it completely contradicted the ethos of "Brotherhood and Unity." Milošević was trying to strengthen centralized rule in the former Yugoslavia, exploiting nationalism to create a "Greater Serbia" that united the Serb-inhabited areas of Croatia and Bosnia and Kosovo, and removing all non-Serbs from these areas through ethnic cleansing. Others say Milošević was more of a political opportunist, driven by a desire for power, seeing himself in the mold of a second Tito, and hijacking nationalist agendas to this end. The different Yugoslav republics split up in a swarm of nationalism, largely stoked by Milošević, who also embraced the historical cult of defeated Serbian grievance that harked back to their humiliation by the Ottoman army in 1389 at the battle of Kosovo Polje in southern Serbia.

But as Croatia, Bosnia, and Slovenia seceded, Yugoslavia collapsed into a hellish, bitter, internecine civil war of nationalism and land-grabbing. Fighting in Croatia broke out in 1991 between the Serb-dominated Yugoslav National Army, local Serbs, and Croatian government forces, after the latter had promptly declared independence from Yugoslavia. Slovenia broke away, Bosnia and Herzegovina declared independence in 1992, and eastern Bosnia and parts of Croatia were partially "ethnically cleansed"[8] of Muslims and Croats by Bosnian Serb and Serb soldiers. Some of them were still operating as part of the old Yugoslav National Army as paramilitaries intent on creating Milošević's ideal. War erupted on European soil for the first time since 1945.

The Bosnian Serb Army, including elements of the former Yugoslav National Army, or JNA, laid siege to Sarajevo from April 1992 to February 1996, a total of nearly four years. It was to be the longest siege of a capital city in modern history. But the city and its staunch defenders never gave in.

Approximately 11,500 people, more than 1,500 of them children, died.[9] This was war fought "amongst the people," as opposed to "between the people," as British paratrooper Lieutenant General Rupert Smith, a UN forces commander in Bosnia, later described it.[10] The opposing armed forces fought their battles in the middle of the movements, refugee fluxes, and daily lives of a civilian population. There were rape camps, ethnic cleansing, concentration camps, forced displacement, and detention centers. In the whole war, 100,000 people died. A million were forced from their homes. Despite massive diplomatic and peacekeeping efforts by Western powers and the international community at large, which proved too often hesitant and ineffectual, the war tore a beautiful country and its singular people into pieces.

In November 1995, an internationally brokered peace treaty hammered out at an airbase in Ohio ended the conflict. Under the auspices of the American diplomat Richard Holbrooke, the different parties agreed to the Dayton Peace Accords, which divided Bosnia into two parts. There was the Muslim-Croat Federation, while the huge Serb-dominated horseshoe of territory stretching around the north and east of the country was established as the Republika Srpska, distinct from the sovereign state of Serbia proper, which lay to the east across the River Drina.

The Muslim-Croat Federation retained its capital in Sarajevo. The war was over, but a vast amount of work had to be done. It was as though the war had taken everybody by surprise, tearing through the country for four years, leaving no time for anything but the present, because nobody during the war knew what was going to happen in the future. Rebuilding Bosnia, stabilizing it, assisting the wounded, burying the dead, and helping the living were the order of the day. Hundreds of millions of dollars, pounds, deutschmarks, and francs poured into the coffers of international development and relief agencies. The war in Bosnia became the top US, NATO, UN, and EU foreign policy priority. Stopping war from breaking out again and keeping the former warring factions apart was paramount. And this was, it must be remembered, December 1995: Americans had seen the mutilated and beaten bodies of US Army Rangers dragged through the dusty streets of Mogadishu in 1993, after a mission to kill or apprehend a Somali warlord, Mohamed Farah Aidid, had gone disastrously wrong. The American public did not want more American soldiers coming back in body bags from a foreign war. Casualties damaged votes: "force protection" for the US soldiers of the Clinton administration was the order of the day.

At the G7 summit held in 1996 in Lyons, then-president Bill Clinton, along with a host of foreign government officials, decided that the bodies of the thousands who had gone missing during the wars in Bosnia and Croatia had to be found, identified, and returned to their relatives. The officials' intention was not just to salve the massive, raw wound of human loss, however. The missing bodies of Srebrenica victims, and thousands of others, threatened to inflame political nationalism and reignite wars. Officials hoped that accounting for the missing would help solve the region's ongoing problem of national violence and would prevent any further outbreak of conflict.

Indeed, the Balkans have never been short of political nationalists. During World War II, for instance, tens of thousands of prisoners, mainly Serbs, Jews, and Roma, had been slaughtered by the Croat nationalist Ustashe at the concentration camp network at Jasenovac in what was then independent Croatia. The number of people who were killed was hotly disputed: some said 75,000 to 100,000, some said many more. The Serb deaths at the camp were reportedly one of the incentives used by Serb forces 50 years later to invade Croatia and take bitter revenge.

Thus, several things needed to be done in 1995 to keep the peace in Bosnia, including the implementation of security guaranteed by NATO soldiers; the rebuilding of the government, making sure that war criminals had no place in it; elections; the return of refugees to their homes; the rebuilding of the country's economy, schools, hospitals, and infrastructure; and the implementation of the rule of law to guarantee justice for war criminals. Dealing with the problem of missing persons was essential to this last effort.

Clinton's initiative to resolve the missing persons issue in the Balkans led to the creation of an organization called the International Commission on Missing Persons. As stated in its mandate, the ICMP would "help Balkans [*sic*] governments deal with the enormous problem of persons who had been killed or had gone missing as a result of wars, ethnic conflicts, human-rights abuses, and humanitarian and natural disasters." The ICMP and its operations in the former Yugoslavia, where some 30,000[11] people had gone missing during the conflicts in Bosnia alone, were to blend together forensic science, human rights, and, most crucially, DNA technology into a world-class formula. Most of the victims were of large-scale massacres, ethnic cleansing operations, concentration camps, mass killings, and the internecine waves of conflict that had characterized the breakup of the six Yugoslav republics from 1991 to 1999.[12]

In particular, the Srebrenica massacre in 1995 required the ICMP's DNA laboratory system to prove itself by solving what a Canadian scientist called "the world's greatest forensic puzzle." Eight thousand one hundred people in total were eventually to be reported missing following the fall of Srebrenica. This was the figure used by the ICMP, the International Committee of the Red Cross (ICRC), the missing persons commissions in the Muslim-Croat Federation and the Republika Srpska, human rights groups, and family associations of victims' relatives. There are 206 bones in a human adult skeleton. If anything approaching 8,000 people were killed, there would be, in theory, as many as 1,668,000 bones to be found, dug up, sorted, and identified. In fact, the skeletons and assorted body parts, and mangled pieces of human body, were spread over dozens of primary and secondary mass graves related to Srebrenica, all scattered over 300-odd square miles of wooded, mountainous eastern Bosnia. The forensic exhumation teams would search a landscape covered in ravines, gorges, and thick slopes forested with pines, as well as undulating fields and pastures. It was country in which, in the words of a forensic scientist, you could bury a town unnoticed. And the Serbs had effectively done just that.

Bosnia in 1995 was no longer as it had been before the war, switch nor would it ever be. There was to be no returning to the halcyon times of the 1984 Olympic Games. There were fewer gray areas—things seemed black or white, good or bad, or just dead or alive. The conflict had left thousands of poor, jobless, unemployable, traumatized, broken, frightened, and angry Bosnians. The war had deeply involved the civilian population at every level; it was not merely a conflict between different armies. There were paramilitary units, ad hoc militias, and military police forces. The kings, queens, castles, and knights that directed and fought the war stamped mercilessly across a chessboard that was the country of Bosnia itself, paying little heed to the civilian pawns trampled underfoot. The main conflicts between 1991 and 1995 were fought in Croatia (1991–1992) and then Bosnia (1992–1995). The latter was a war fought by three sides across multiple and constantly changing front lines largely inside one country, the territory of Bosnia and Herzegovina. The civilian population had little choice: they stayed put and suffered, they fled as refugees, they fought, or they died. Bosnians had frighteningly little control over their fate during the war, and too little afterward.

One hundred thousand of them died. A million were forced from their homes. There were 30,000 cases of missing persons. By 1996 some estimates showed that a quarter to a third of the population was suffering from trauma-related illnesses. The fact that for many Bosnians life before the war had been stable and comfortable, that the war took them by surprise, and that it was riveted with incidents of extreme brutality and hardship contributed to the deep trauma civilians experienced. Thousands of families by the war's end had a missing relative—a son, brother, or father who had been executed, taken away at night, or simply disappeared, vanished into the fog of war. These relatives of the missing needed help coming to terms with what had happened, moving toward the future, picking up the pieces, and putting the past to bed.

Following the Bosnian government's request for help, the newly created ICMP began working on the problem of missing persons by reuniting these families with the human remains of the dead. For the thousands of mothers, daughters, aunts, and grandmothers who had lost their menfolk at Srebrenica and in other places during the war (the dead ranged from teenagers to those in their eighties), the last ten to fifteen years had been full of mental anguish—of not knowing, of waiting, and of living with dashed hopes, false rumors, and misleading reports as they waited to hear news and find out the truth of what exactly had happened.

It was a quest for justice too. The quest for the remains of victims dovetailed with the hunt for evidence about the perpetrators: locating the mass graves, the secret burial sites, the dumping grounds for the thousands of bodies and body parts often meant finding information that could lead to triggermen, and in turn to those who had commanded the execution squads and given the orders.

At the top, the Bosnian Serb military units and sub-units that had, according to The Hague Tribunal's indictments,[13] carried out the killings at Srebrenica had been commanded by Colonel General Ratko Mladić. In July 1995 Mladić was indicted for war crimes and genocide by the ICTY, the internationally established court set up by the UN in 1993 to deal with war criminals allegedly responsible for crimes that had taken place across the former Yugoslavia. The tribunal had already indicted people from all sides, including senior commanders, by the time the war ended. Forensic operations to dig up the victims of executions and other war crimes in Bosnia started almost as soon as the war finished: at first the evidence was used to prove fact of death. But then the ICMP, once it had been established, saw the urgent need to identify the thousands of human remains and return them to their families for proper burial. Some of the perpetrators, once submitted to judicial process and the law, gave up information that, once obtained, could be used to locate the places where the victims had been buried. In helping the relatives in their desperate quest to find the missing, the ICMP's technology would develop, evolve, and become more and more effective as the years after the Bosnian war unfolded.

The ICMP also strengthened the rule of law and human rights by forming family associations of victims' relatives who could press for such things as legal rights. Its operations were part of a kind of human rights and forensic science "double whammy." This was made all the more effective because it took place at the same time as existing DNA-assisted identification technology was being developed, after it became clear that so-called "traditional" methods used in Central and South America and the Balkans prior to 2000—including identifying missing persons' remains by personal items found on the bodies like false teeth, identity papers, and jewelry, as well as dental records, clothing, and fingerprints—were often flawed, unreliable, and inadequate. All of this happened in the early years after the war as Bosnia was under partial international administration, with an international pro consul from the Office of the High Representative, established to carry out the implementation of the Dayton Peace Accords, and with thousands of NATO soldiers deployed as peacekeepers in the country.

And so, coming out of the Srebrenica massacre, the ICMP developed a new human rights–based approach and a scientific methodology including the key use of forensic anthropology and archaeology for finding, excavating, and exhuming the remains of thousands of bodies of the victims from mass graves. Then, afterward, scientists employed DNA technology to identify the remains of these victims. As a result of these breakthroughs, a groundbreaking, internationally funded laboratory system was set up in Bosnia, mainly staffed by Bosnians. Today, it is a world leader in the field and an international scientific success story for the country.

The laboratory system is so precise that information gathered is requested for use as material evidence in war crimes trials in The Hague. This successful approach to identifying missing persons has led leaders from Iraq to Colombia to request the assistance of the ICMP. The organization has also become one of the world leaders in Disaster Victim Identification, which means the methods have proven useful following Hurricane Katrina, the Asian tsunami, and other natural disasters.

The ICMP initially aimed to identify victims so that living relatives found some comfort and resolution. But by connecting victims' families and helping form victims' relatives into family associations, tangential benefits appeared: family members organized to push for new laws and pressured governments on such issues as social, economic, and legal rights. Crucially, as stated above, the material evidence, in the form of the DNA matches the ICMP made over the years, was requested as evidence by both the prosecution and defense in war crimes trials in The Hague. Eventually, the evidence of crimes gathered through forensic, investigatory, judicial, and other methods would help establish a form of accountability that applied to dictators, warlords, and war criminals from countries in the Balkans to Africa, the Middle East, and elsewhere. The message was clear: the human remains of their victims could be found and identified and could, one day, come back to haunt the perpetrators in court. This was the case in the Balkans and later would emerge onto a wider, twenty-first-century stage of history, justice, reconciliation, and forensic science.

Finding out the inside story of how the world's greatest forensic science puzzle was solved, how the hunt for alleged war criminals like Ratko Mladić was carried out, and how such vital imperatives as justice and reconciliation were implemented is a matter of talking to the right people. It's a matter of knowledge, contacts, and trust. These persons—Bosnians, Americans, Serbs, Britons, French, Germans, good, bad, and neutral—are the tips of their respective icebergs of influence. Gain their trust, and they'll recommend you onward, to those who were *really* there. Those who exhumed the mass graves, who saw the signals memos, who actually wrote the reports, who were on the helicopters, who gave the orders, who did the surveillance, who attended the meetings, who *were* in the know, and, sometimes, who *actually* pulled the triggers.

Srebrenica's story starts with the forensic staff and investigators from the ICTY and later the ICMP who were on the forensic front lines. They dug up—and in the ICMP's case continue to dig up—the mass graves containing the victims. The ICMP developed and worked in the laboratories where the DNA matching systems were put into place. They, along with the crucial organizations of family members of the victims of the Srebrenica massacre, the human rights and legal apparatus, and their proponents and implementers who furthered their cause were gold mines of information. For example, the judiciary and prosecutorial staff of the ICTY gave some information about exactly what happened at Srebrenica and what the perpetrators did afterward. And they can tell how former general Ratko Mladić hid for so long, was caught, and was put on trial, and how the evidence against him and his cohorts was gathered.

Only after meeting with these people, listening to their stories, and finding out what they did and what happened to them can one tell the story of Srebrenica, of Bosnia's million bones, of the world's largest forensic science puzzle, and of how science and human rights came together to help Bosnia and other countries deal with the past and

confront the future. The story spotlights the crucial issues of reconciliation, peace and security, transitional justice, advanced forensic science,
and the application of human rights and rule of law.

Many of the people who have the necessary information in this story
work for what is widely known as "The International Community." This
is an enormous professional conglomerate of thousands of political,
economic, military, judicial, media, law enforcement, diplomatic, and
humanitarian staff and personnel. They work in countries such as Iraq,
Libya, Bosnia, the Democratic Republic of the Congo, and many others
on a huge variety of different missions that can range from peacekeeping and peace support to humanitarian aid, rule of law enforcement,
ceasefire monitoring, and nation-state building. The organizations they
work for include NATO, the United Nations' different agencies, the various missions deployed by the European Union to conflict and post-
conflict areas, and the countless relief and medical aid staff working on
humanitarian deployments. The international community also includes
journalists, experts working for think tanks like the International Crisis
Group, and human rights monitors from Human Rights Watch and
Amnesty International. They concentrate on tracking and reporting
human rights abuses and trying to make a world of war and rampant
injustice a slightly safer and more accountable place.

In places from Kosovo to Libya, and from Haiti to Somalia and
Afghanistan, there are diplomats representing multiple countries ranging from the United States to Australia and Pakistan. There are soldiers
from countries like the United Kingdom, Canada, and Estonia deployed
on NATO missions. There are surgeons and anesthetists from Holland
and France working for Doctors Without Borders in famine camps in
South Sudan, and in the combat areas in the Caucasus where medical
facilities are hard-stretched, non existent, or destroyed. There are police
officers from countries like Argentina, say, or Norway or South Africa, on
missions to train police forces in developing and post-conflict countries.

The international community is made up of people from half the countries on earth. In Kosovo in 1999, for instance, 41 different nationalities of soldiers and police officers were deployed on NATO and UN military and police missions to keep the peace in the southern Serbian province after the 1999 NATO bombing campaign of Yugoslavia had ended.[14] All of these different individuals from the international community live, work, and operate in countries that lie between war and development, self-determination, and self-government, often in a kind of administrative limbo where the international community takes over to keep the peace, build a state, or stave off a humanitarian disaster. These individuals are often in the right, sometimes partially so, and sometimes in the wrong.

In this world, everybody seems to know everybody else, which makes it an ideal network from which to procure information. The participants at a work meeting in the office at three in the afternoon will often go on to gather around a restaurant table later that evening. Everybody was based somewhere before and everybody's going on to somewhere else: today is Iraq; tomorrow is Syria. Yesterday was Burundi; before that was Mali. The sand of political economic urgency and diplomatic expediency moves quickly through the international hourglass these days. And what was learned—or not—on previous international deployments is passed on to the next mission, the next crisis, the next country.

So, when it comes to Srebrenica and missing persons, the first people to meet are the forensic archaeologists who exhume the bullet-riddled detritus of human wreckage from mass graves and the forensic anthropologists who put the shattered skeletons back together again. Then there are the geneticists and DNA analysts who make DNA matches on the human remains. After this, human rights officers come in to assist in dealing with the families of the dead victims. Going forward, there are war crimes investigators, judges, international and regional police officers, lawyers for defense and prosecution, and crucially, thousands of relatives of dead victims of war crimes, the survivors and families left behind after the tide of war washed out one last time, leaving them high and dry.

The wars that tore apart the former Yugoslavia at the beginning of the nineties seem like a long time ago now. 9/11, Iraq, and Afghanistan have intervened. Presidents and prime ministers across the world change, international justice moves forward, countries at war make peace, economic recession washes across continents. Arab countries have revolutions. Civil war and insurgency breaks out in Syria. But to find out how the world really began to deal with missing persons, it is necessary to start with the investigators, scientists, and families of Srebrenica victims. It means starting with the events that took place one summer nearly twenty years ago in a small and beautiful valley in eastern Bosnia—events that were to become the epicenter of the world of missing persons.

Chapter Two

SEPARATING THE MEN FROM THE WOMEN AND CHILDREN IN SREBRENICA

Kada Hotic, a Bosnian Muslim, was fifty in 1995, the last year she would see her son, her husband, and her two brothers alive. She had lived much of her life in the former silver-mining town of Srebrenica, set in a verdant and fertile valley close to the Drina River in the mountain woods of eastern Bosnia. Kada and her husband, Sejad, a sociology professor also from Srebrenica, were surprised by the start of the war in Bosnia in 1992. The Bosnian Serb Army (VRS) had occupied or ethnically cleansed most of the Bosnian Muslims and Croats in much of eastern Bosnia in the opening months of the war. Srebrenica and the land around it held out as a pocket defended by Bosnian Muslim soldiers and filled with Bosnian Muslim civilians. From 1992 onward, the defenders of this pocket and the Bosnian Serb forces around it conducted a series of tit-for-tat attacks on each other's positions and centers of residence. Often the casualties were civilian.

By the time Kada and her family realized how the war was progressing, in 1992, it was too late to leave Srebrenica. Barricades manned by *Chetniks* (Serbian irregular soldiers) surrounded the city, and the shooting never seemed to stop. Muslim houses in the town were torched during one attack; Serb houses were left alone. She spent eleven nights in a row with 56 members of her family, hiding in the snowy woods while the

Serbs trashed and looted their homes. Muslims were shot in front of the police station. People in wheelchairs were burned alive in their homes. Muslim refugees from surrounding areas flooded into the enclave.

Srebrenica was cut off from the rest of Bosnia quite early in the war. It lay very close to the border with Serbia to the east, and it lay in an isolated rural valley. As early as late 1992 and early 1993 it was effectively surrounded, although its population of refugees from Bosnian Serb attacks in surrounding areas grew as the war went on. A variety of units from UNPROFOR, or the United Nations Protection Force, the UN mission in Bosnia, had been successively deployed there. At the end of 1994 and the very beginning of 1995, a Dutch unit drawn from an airmobile brigade had a desperately difficult assignment, since the troops were caught between the pressures of those in the enclave who demanded to be defended, the surrounding Bosnian Serb forces, and the multilayered and bureaucratic UN mandate. Despite the seemingly impossible constraints, the peacekeepers, including a Canadian battalion sent there before the Dutch, did their best. The Dutch recognized the desperate situation they were in and made repeated requests for assistance. However, it is clear what some of the Dutch troops thought of the Bosnian Muslim refugees: one piece of graffiti left on the walls of their barracks outside Srebrenica, scrawled in black letters and still visible today, reads: "No teeth? Mustache? Smell like shit? Bosnian girl!"

The Bosnians were terrified of being left to their fate by the UN. Srebrenica's people, protected by Bosnian Muslim army units commanded by Naser Orić, seemed to hold the Dutch airmobile unit responsible for all of the UN's indecisiveness and operational shortcomings in Bosnia. There were many of these—sometimes, it seemed to Bosnians, too many to count. Sometimes hardest for them to understand was that the UN was a protection force, under a constrictive mandate. Its complex rules of engagement meant that its ability to return fire, protect civilians, and curtail aggression by all three sides was limited. The Serbs saw them as an obstacle to their occupation of Srebrenica, one of three enclaves in eastern Bosnia (along with Goražde and Žepa) that continued to hold out against them. The three enclaves were defended by irregular fighters and by the national Army of Bosnia and Herzegovina (ABIH), made up predominantly of Muslims and Croats.[1]

The VRS said the armed occupants of the enclaves were responsible for civilian casualties in neighboring Serb-held villages. They had a point. For instance, on Orthodox Christmas Day, January 7, 1993, the village of Kravica, near Srebrenica, was attacked by forces based in the enclave. They killed Bosnian Serb civilians and military and destroyed homes in the village. The number of civilians killed was hotly disputed, but the attack, and others, would lead to the indictment by The Hague Tribunal of Naser Orić on charges related to killings in and around the enclave.[2]

Regardless of the casualty figures, the attack further strengthened the enormous and lethal antagonism between both sides. There was little or no food in cut-off Srebrenica, and many people were close to starvation.

"Everybody looked the same," Kada Hotic was to say later. "All identical, with these big, dark, hungry, staring eyes."[3] Some people slept on the freezing streets. Even relief efforts proved dangerous. A French doctor, Georges Dallemagne, working with Doctors Without Borders, said he had seen the corpses of two people who were crushed and killed when crates of air-dropped US relief supplies fell on them at night. He also noted that only the strongest received any aid—those who pushed and shoved secured the necessary supplies and shelter—while 5,000 people were left living on the streets.[4] General Philippe Morillon, the four-star French general who was then the commander of the UN Protection Force troops in Bosnia, upped the ante when he visited the enclave in March 1993. He was so shocked by what he saw that he decided to stay for a full week: the UN flag was raised on the town hall to a cheering crowd of

Muslims, and UN blue-helmeted soldiers from the Canadian battalion who were stationed in the town. Morillon declared on amateur radio:

> Fully conscious that a major tragedy was about to take place in Srebrenica, I deliberately came here and I have now decided to stay here in order to calm the anguish of the population and to save them, or to try to save them. To the population of Srebrenica, I say, don't be afraid, I shall be with you.

Kada Hotic remembers him visiting the town. She recalls that when a UN convoy departed with Morillon at the end of his stay, a mother placed a dead child in front of one of the armored personnel carriers to try and prevent it from leaving. Crucially, by staying in the enclave for a week, the French general had negotiated the safe entry from Serbia, along icy, mined roads, of a seventeen-truck humanitarian aid convoy, whose eighty tons of aid kept the beleaguered outpost alive for a few more weeks. The surrounding Bosnian Serb forces were outraged: they had not allowed any aid into the enclave since the previous December, because they were accusing the Army of Bosnia and Herzegovina of using Srebrenica as a staging post from which to launch attacks on the surrounding Serb-held territory. Muhamed Sacirbey, Bosnia's ambassador to the UN, said simply: "Thank God for General Morillon. We have had many differences with him. But it seems that one man with a blue helmet has more commitment and guts than the entire United Nations." These words tempted a vengeful fate.

On Orthodox Christmas in 1994, a group of inhabitants from Srebrenica, including Kada Hotic, gathered together for a nocturnal food raid into the neighboring hamlet of Kravica, pulling makeshift sledges through the snow-covered fields of dead maize that lay in the valley. Even a twelve-year-old girl whose mother could not get out of bed went on this raid, accompanied by a few of the Bosnian Muslim men who had guns. The expedition netted sixty kilos of maize, half of which was carried on their backs, the other half in plastic beer crates. It would keep them from starvation for just a bit longer.[5]

By early 1995, the enclaves in eastern Bosnia, the three so-called "safe havens" of Žepa, Goražde, and Srebrenica, had become an enormous problem for all sides. The war had been going on for four years, the country was on the evening news internationally on a continuous basis, and it was a foreign policy priority for the United States and Europe. Despite all this attention, however, Bosnia's extraordinarily complex war had made physical access to enclaves like Srebrenica almost impossible, and it was as if the parts of the country were completely cut off from the rest of the world.

Meanwhile, outside the former Yugoslavia other foreign crises mounted. In 1995, the world was still reeling from the First Gulf War, which sent thousands of American, British, and European troops into action in Kuwait and Iraq. The Rwandan genocide had taken place a year earlier. Ebola stalked Zaire. Russian troops were fighting in Chechnya. Israel's prime minister Yitzhak Rabin was assassinated that November.

In the self-contained world of Bosnia, which was consuming so much international attention, NATO and UN commanders wanted to end the war. They were encouraged in this by the highly experienced and operationally perspicacious British paratrooper Lieutenant General Rupert Smith, then-commander of the UN peacekeeping forces, who wanted to finally broker a peace deal. Smith was keen to achieve this by bringing in the American-dominated NATO air capacity and, if necessary, bombing the Bosnian Serbs into submission. He aimed to support this attack by deploying a rapid reaction force to Bosnia. These soldiers would not be controlled by the same constrictive rules of engagement as those suffocating the UNPROFOR troops.

Yasushi Akashi, a Japanese career diplomat who was UN Secretary-General Boutros-Boutros Ghali's special representative in the country, instituted the mandates emanating from the UN's headquarters in New York, but he and General Smith and the NATO staff acknowledged that if airstrikes were ordered, the UN troops in the enclaves—the British in Goražde, the Dutch in Srebrenica—would become instant targets if they were not withdrawn before the attacks began. The Bosnian Muslims feared the worst if the UN troops left. They knew the Serbs wanted the Muslim population removed, or simply displaced somewhere else, back into territory controlled by their own side, so that there would be no Muslim outposts left in the territory after the peace deal. If the UN troops departed, the civilian population in the enclaves would at best become displaced people locked in enemy territory that humanitarian organizations could not reach. At worst, they could be slaughtered.

By this stage of the war, too, many feared a Croatian military offensive in the west of Bosnia that would retake Croat territory in the Krajina area lost to the Serbs early in the war. Colonel General Ratko Mladić, commander of the main staff of the Bosnian Serb Army, worried that his area of command in eastern Bosnia, which contained the enclaves, would be overlooked by the Bosnian Serb political leadership in the event of a Croat offensive in the west. Essentially, the war was ending and the Bosnian Serbs wanted to hold on to as much of their territory as they could. They knew that at forthcoming peace talks territory occupied by their troops was land they stood a better chance of keeping, and they wanted territory in eastern Bosnia that abutted Serbia proper.

Mladić's forces had also been laying siege to the Bosnian capital, Sarajevo, for nearly four years. Thousands of people, mostly civilians, had been killed, but the city, and its tenacious civilian inhabitants, still held out. Meanwhile, far to the east and south of Srebrenica, other problems were surfacing. Lieutenant Colonel Jonathon Riley, the determined and adept British commander of the battalion of the Royal Welch Fusiliers based in Goražde, was focused on fulfilling his mission, but he was also determined to get all of his men home alive from Bosnia.[6] Not only would this leave the Bosnian Muslim enclave terribly vulnerable to Bosnian Serb attack, it would prove difficult to orchestrate.

By early 1995 the Bosnian Serb Army was not Riley's major problem. Instead, he was focused on the Bosnian Muslims. Led by Brigadier Hamid Bahto, the Bosnian Muslims threatened to kill the British peacekeepers if they tried to pull out. The enclaves had become thorns in everyone's sides. The situation was further complicated by Mladić's meeting in June with French general Bernard Janvier, commander of UN forces in Yugoslavia, who was seeking the release of UN hostages, many of whom were French. As a bargaining chip, Mladić demanded that the 1994 NATO airstrikes not be repeated. But even in this tempestuous climate, nobody could have foreseen the outcome of the situation in the enclaves.

British defense analyst Tim Ripley was then a journalist based in the United Kingdom, making frequent trips to Bosnia, researching and analyzing the last year of the Bosnian war. (His definitive work would eventually be published as *Operation Deliberate Force*, titled after the code name for the 1995 NATO airstrikes.) According to Ripley, nobody in Sarajevo expected the men from Srebrenica to be killed; it was assumed that Mladić would simply take them prisoner and exchange them for captured Bosnian Serb soldiers, as had been common practice for both sides since the outbreak of war.[7]

But on a sweltering July 11, 1995, after days of shelling, the Dutch UN peacekeepers in Potočari failed to prevent Mladić's forces from entering the Srebrenica enclave. Bosnian Serb forces took a number of peacekeepers hostage and stole their weapons, radios, uniforms, and equipment. Mladić's men tore into Srebrenica and the neighboring village of Potočari, crowded by this point with some 45,000 starving Bosnian Muslims. Mladić's forces separated the men of Srebrenica from the women and children, and packed the latter onto buses to be driven back to safe territory controlled by Muslim and Croat enemies.[8] When the words "separating the men from the women and children" are heard in a Balkans conflict, history has proven that mass atrocities are to come.

The men were taken away. In an atmosphere of horrorstruck rumors, sweating panic, and running terror, Mladić's Serbs spread out into Srebrenica and Potočari. They were supported by a barrage of anti-aircraft cannon shelling and tracer bullets.

Meanwhile, the beleaguered Dutch, desperately outgunned and convinced they were being left to their fate by the higher echelons of NATO and the UN, made repeated calls for NATO airstrikes to support them; there were no less than six requests logged between July 6 and 11. They could do little to staunch the shelling or the Serb armored vehicles pouring into the enclave. But despite the inevitability of the enclave's fall, requests for air support had to crawl up the multilayered chain of command, from Srebrenica to Tuzla to Sarajevo to Zagreb, and thence on to air force units in Italy or on seaborne carriers. On the morning of July 11, UNPROFOR's Sector North-East in Tuzla asked the Dutch battalion in Srebrenica to resubmit their fifth request, as it had been sent on the wrong form. Despite the fact that the demands for help got more and more urgent, no airstrikes were yet approved, and Mladić's Serbs shelled, approached, and finally entered the enclave.

When airstrikes were finally dispatched on the afternoon of July 11, two Dutch F-16s swooped in and dropped two 250-kilo bombs on Serb armored vehicles. The two aircraft were the vanguard of a much-larger NATO strike force bound for Srebrenica. Lieutenant Manja Blok, the first female fighter pilot in the Koninklijke Luchtmacht, the Royal Netherlands Air Force, flew one of the F-16s. She described the moment she dropped a bomb on a Serb tank.

> *Controller (Head-up Display, or HUD)*: Roger, take the second hairpin turn, there's a
> tank firing at our position, everything that you see on that road direction south, is
> cleared hot for you. Did you copy, over?

Blok (HUD): Roger copied, confirm cleared hot....OK, setting up for the attack.

Controller (HUD): If you see a big antenna, near to it is also a tank, over.

Blok (HUD): OK, I see that one the right part after the turn. Between the houses with
    the red roofs and the turn I see tanks, confirm?

Controller (HUD): Roger, give 'em hell!

Blok (HUD): Roger, coming in![9]

Afterward, the Dutch pilots stressed that they wished they could have dropped more than the two bombs. However, Mladić knew from substantial experience the way to twist the international community's decision-making arm. He took some 30 Dutch soldiers hostage and let it be known that if airstrikes continued the Dutchmen would die. The Dutch commander reportedly informed his government of the situation in the enclave. Airstrikes ceased. Srebrenica fell.

That first night Kada Hotic remembers the nonstop shooting and screams as Serbs roamed the streets of Srebrenica. On July 13, she and her husband, along with thousands of other panicked refugees, tried to walk to the Dutch UN base in the abandoned battery factory in the adjacent town of Potočari. The Dutch soldiers were deciding whom to let in. The situation was chaotic. Serbs were rounding up prisoners and had already begun individual executions away from the UN base. The Dutch soldiers were on the receiving end of a vast wave of people seeking sanctuary at their base: the beleaguered UN soldiers, overwhelmed by the Serbs, did nothing to stop the soldiers from preventing any men from entering the compound. The Serbs were almost in complete control.

One of Kada's brothers had already been taken away—she found out later that he was tortured before being killed—and many of the other men had already set off across the hills trying to break out of the enclave and get to safety. At the entrance to the Dutch base, a Serb soldier pushed a gun into the side of her husband's neck and pushed him aside. He had a rucksack with him, with the pictures from their whole family's life in it.

As she watched him being dragged away, Kada thought, "Why am I not taking the rucksack with the pictures with me?"

That was the last time she saw her husband. Kada and the other women and girls from Srebrenica were forced onto buses and driven across the front line to the town of Tuzla, territory held by the Bosnian Army. Riding out of Srebrenica, she saw Serb soldiers lining the side of the road, giving them three-fingered nationalist salutes. There were dead bodies in the hamlets of Konjević Polje and in Kravica, and the Bosnian Muslim men who had been captured were standing at the roadside. When the buses got to Nova Kasaba, they saw a huge group of men sitting on the football field, the same men that Madeleine Albright saw in her aerial photos before they vanished.

General Ratko Mladić, meanwhile, had already left Srebrenica for Belgrade. He had a meeting on July 15 with the UN Protection Force's General Smith and his military assistant, Lieutenant Colonel Jim Baxter, to discuss the situation in the other enclave, Goražde, that lay twenty miles south down the Drina River. Goražde was, at that point, still occupied by around 300 British UN peacekeepers, and Mladić wanted them out of the way so he could concentrate on taking over this pinprick of land, controlled by Bosnian Muslims and the international community, that had resisted his Bosnian Serb forces for nearly three years. He left his subordinates to oversee the ongoing Operation Krivaja 95: the deployments in, toward, and around the enclaves of Srebrenica and Žepa.

At midnight on July 11, a huge column formed of Bosnian Muslim men from the Srebrenica enclave. The procession was comprised of some 5,500 to 6,000 Bosnian Muslim soldiers, some armed, some not, accompanied by approximately 7,000 male civilians. The column was seven to ten miles long, moving in single file in some places, and its aim was to simply march through Bosnian Serb lines to Tuzla, nearly 30 miles away and the nearest point under the control of the Army of Bosnia and Herzegovina. The marchers, desperately short of food and water, and emaciated after months and years in the Srebrenica enclave, were ill clad (some wore plastic bags around their feet in place of boots), dehydrated, disorientated, terrified, and starving. Many of the armed men had no ammunition, and the column's chances of success seemed slim. By the time the first members of the column crossed over the asphalt road that led from the village of Konjević Polje to the town of Bratunac, Bosnian Serb forces had already ambushed the group. Artillery, mortar, anti-aircraft, and small-arms fire had split the column in many places. Some of the men in their traumatized state, dehydrated, hypoglycemic, and starving, killed themselves or others. The Serbs had, in some cases, donned stolen UN uniforms from the Dutch. They convinced captured men from the column to go back into the woods and persuade the hundreds of others to come out.

From the outset, the level of violence inflicted by the Bosnian Serbs made it clear what the fate of the Muslim male prisoners would be. One man surrendered to the Serbs and witnessed several dozen of his colleagues being machine-gunned; he was sent back to find other members of the column. When he rejoined his compatriots, they saw what the Serbs had done to him: one of his eyes was gouged out, his ears were cut off, and an (Orthodox) cross was carved into his forehead.[10]

A breakaway portion of the column, comprised mostly of armed soldiers, managed to break through Bosnian Serb lines and fight their way to Tuzla. Muhamed Duraković, one of the Bosnian Muslim Srebrenica men who decided that it would be better to try to flee through the forests rather than take refuge at the Dutch UN base in Potočari, was twenty years old. When asked later to recount his memories of life before the war, he described Srebrenica as a small industrial town where everyone knew everyone else. He described a wonderful childhood there, not just because, as he said, he lived in the best place in the whole world, but because of the simplicity of life and the laid-back mentality, free of any worry.[11] He loved animals, and as his father was a hunter, they always had at least one dog. Sometimes they had two or more, and it was the young Duraković's job to attend to their needs—as he said, the best job a boy can have. He had many friends, too; living in a small community taught him to get to know and appreciate everyone, and he built solid friendships that he believed would last him for a lifetime.

Then the war began.

He'd spent the war inside Srebrenica, and when it came to the final moment to leave, he said goodbye to his family's house, walked with his father across the garden he knew so well, and went down through the waving, hot fields of summer grass to the forest's edge. There, they started to run. Their journey through the forests lasted 37 days, during which time they watched their friends and colleagues die in minefields, from lack of food or water, or from being shot by Bosnian Serb soldiers. Duraković says that they were "like deer trying to flee the wolves."[12] (Among the first Serbs into Srebrenica were fighters of a mobile combat unit named, somewhat appropriately, the Drina Wolves.)

Duraković managed to reach the Bosnian Army–controlled territory near the town of Kladanj. He still remembers the face of the first friendly soldier that he met at the front line. Duraković stumbled toward him in his civilian jacket and dark blue trousers, completely worn out, and the soldier, in his camouflage uniform, looked at him as if he had seen a ghost. Later that day Duraković was picked up by a bus and taken to a place called Živinice. At first he was ecstatic. Before he asked for food or drink, he grabbed a phone inside a barber's shop and called his mother, trapped in Sarajevo, to let her know that he was alive. And then it hit him. He realized that he had survived when so many had not. He fell, he says, into a deep depression from which it took years to recover. Nevertheless, he was alive. Thousands of men from Srebrenica had not been so lucky.

On the afternoon of July 11, 1995, General Ratko Mladić, along with other Bosnian Serb Army and civilian envoys, met in the Hotel Fontana in Bratunac, a few miles from Srebrenica, with Dutch military officers and representatives of the Bosnian Muslim refugees from Potočari.[13] At this meeting, Mladić explained to the group that he would supervise the transportation of refugees from Potočari and wanted to screen all the Bosnian Muslim males between approximately age 16 and 60 as possible war criminals.[14] He also issued threats against the Dutch soldiers, including those in captivity. An estimated 9,000 Bosnian Muslim soldiers and civilians were to be left behind in the Srebrenica enclave to be captured over the succeeding days.

On July 13, soldiers rounded up some 6,000 Bosnian Muslims[15] outside Srebrenica on the road from Bratunac to Konjević Polje and took them to the football field at Nova Kasaba, a small nearby hamlet. It was there that the American U2 aircraft caught them with their photo-reconnaissance cameras. The images taken from tens of thousands of feet in the air do not, and cannot, show the terrified lines of men, many of them barefoot, stripped to the waist, as they sat and waited for what came next. They were sweating and emaciated. Bosnian Serb TV footage of these men on that day shows men malnourished and thin thanks to months and years of living inside Srebrenica on near-starvation rations. Before they were moved from the football field, the prisoners had two visits from General Mladić, who assured them that they would be treated as prisoners of war and almost certainly exchanged for Bosnian Serbs being held captive by the Army of Bosnia and Herzegovina. Soldiers then took the men away in trucks and on the same buses that had been used to transport the women and children from Srebrenica to the safety of territory occupied by the Army of Bosnia and Herzegovina.[16]

Between 1,000 and 1,500 of the men were taken to the Agricultural Cooperative warehouses at Kravica, white-walled buildings by the road that led from Bratunac. A similar number were bused to the Grbavci school in Orahovac, approximately 1,100 to Branjevo Military Farm, 400 to the nearby Kozluk bottling plant, 500 to the cultural center in the village of Pilica, and somewhere between 1,500 to 2,000 to the dam and school at Petkovici. And in between the afternoon of July 14 and dusk on July 16, they were all shot by machine guns. Very few survived.

The River Cerska is a small sub-tributary of the Drina that flows to the west of the village of Konjević Polje; the first mass shootings took place on the afternoon of July 13 on its banks. One witness, hidden among trees, saw two or three trucks followed by an armored vehicle and an earth-moving machine proceeding toward Cerska. After that, he heard gunshots for half an hour and then saw the armored vehicle going in the opposite direction; the earth-moving machine stayed put.[17]

Muhamed Duraković, fleeing with his father, appears to have passed by this execution site later on that day; others reported seeing bodies thrown into a ditch at the side of the road, some of whom were still alive.[18] Aerial photos and excavations later confirmed the presence of a mass grave near this location. The spread of Kalashnikov bullet cases found at the scene showed that the approximately 150 Bosnian male victims were put in a row on one side of the road while the Serb shooters faced them on the other.

Meanwhile, the so-called "dam" at Petkovici stands over a small lake, and it was here that many of those killed at Petkovici were actually shot. On July 14 and 15, soldiers took an estimated 1,500 to 2,000 of the Bosnian Muslim prisoners from a centralized holding area beside the road near the town of Bratunac and transported them to the secondary school in the village of Petkovici. It was boiling hot outside, and inside the cramped rooms of the school it was even hotter. The Bosnian Serb captors did not give the men any food or water, and a group of prisoners reportedly chose to drink their own urine, only worsening their thirst.[19] Stripped to the waist and barefoot, the prisoners had their hands tied behind their backs, and during the night of July 14 they were taken in lorries to the dam at Petkovici, where, as they arrived, they could see what had happened to those who had been brought there before them. Bodies lay strewn on the ground, their hands tied behind their backs. In groups of five to ten men, they were taken out of the trucks, lined up, and shot.[20]

In transcripts of testimony included in the judgment from The Hague trial of former General Radislav Krstić, one survivor described his feelings of overwhelming fear—and overwhelming thirst.

> I was really sorry that I would die thirsty, and I was trying to hide among the people for as long as I could, like everybody else. I just wanted to live for another second or two. And when it was my turn, I jumped out with what I believe were four other people. I could feel the gravel beneath my feet. It hurt. I was walking with my head bent down and I wasn't feeling anything. And then I thought that I would die very fast, that I would not suffer. And I just thought that my mother would never know where I had ended up. This is what I was thinking as I was getting out of the truck. I was still very thirsty. But it was sort of between life and death. I didn't know whether I wanted to live or to die anymore. I decided not to call out for them to shoot and kill me, but I was sort of praying to God that they'd come and kill me. But I decided not to call them and I was waiting to die.[21]

After the executions had finished—a process that took several hours—there were only two survivors. They helped each other untie their hands and then crawled out from under the piles of bodies and decided to try and hide, heading for woods overlooking the lake nearby. The hot summer day had made it perfectly feasible for them to spend the night outside, on a slope overseeing the execution site. When daylight allowed them both to see what was going on, they saw bulldozers collecting the bodies. One of the survivors had also crucially seen Ratko Mladić en route to the scene the previous day.[22]

In the village of Kravica, not far from Srebrenica, an aerial photograph taken at 2:00 p.m. on July 14 shows two large buses outside the Agricultural Cooperative warehouses. At 6:00 p.m. the killing began. Major Dragan Obrenović was then acting as the deputy commander and chief of staff of the First Zvornik Infantry Brigade of the Bosnian Serb Army. In his testimony to The Hague Tribunal, Obrenović claims that the killing started when some of the Muslim prisoners started to fight back against their guards and even grabbed hold of one and killed him.[23] In reaction, the other Serb soldiers guarding the men opened fire with assault rifles and threw hand grenades, after which nearly a thousand Bosnian Muslim men, the youngest of them merely teenagers and the eldest a disabled man in his seventies, were pushed into the crumbling building. The Serb soldiers then walked into the entrance as the afternoon sun cast shadows behind them and fired magazine after magazine from their Kalashnikovs. The soldiers threw in hand grenades, and part of the building was set on fire. An anti-tank rocket was even fired at the Muslims. Reportedly, the local Serb population participated in the killings as well, as some of the victims were mutilated and killed with knives. Kravica was the village near Srebrenica that had been the target of the attack by Naser Orić's men from inside the enclave in January 1993, in which Bosnian Serb civilians had been killed. The civilians most likely wanted vengeance.

On the same day, a former member of the Bratunac Brigade, who by then worked as the director of an agricultural cooperative in Bratunac, drove to the warehouses to check on the sales of a consignment of raspberries. When he arrived, he saw masked VRS soldiers at the far end of the warehouse. They were lining men up, ordering them to lie on the ground, and then shooting them in the backs of their heads, a process they were calling "vaccinations" in shouted conversations with each other. The men who were left alive were then shot in the back, underneath the left shoulder blade.[24] The man shouted at the soldiers, and they turned their guns on him, but a fellow agricultural cooperative worker intervened, along with some Kravica villagers.

The bodies were then taken to Bratunac or were simply dumped in the river that runs alongside the road or piled into large mass graves close by. Between July 11 and 19, within a twenty-mile radius of Srebrenica, some 7,500 people were slaughtered. There were three survivors of the slaughter in the farm sheds at Kravica. One, slightly wounded, recounted what happened:

> I was not even able to touch the floor, the concrete floor of the building....After the shooting, I felt a strange kind of heat, warmth, which was actually coming from the blood that covered the concrete floor, and I was stepping on the dead people who were lying around. But there were even people who were still alive, who were only wounded, and as soon as I would step on one, I would hear him cry, moan, because I was trying to move as fast as I could. I could tell that people had been completely disembodied, and I could feel bones of the people that had been hit by those bursts of gunfire or shells, I could feel their ribs crushing. And then I would get up again and continue.[25]

This survivor climbed out of a window and tried to run across the fields behind the warehouse. He was seen and shot at by a guard but then pretended to be dead. Another survivor spent the night under a pile of bodies and watched the following morning as Serb soldiers examined the bodies for signs of life. The indictments filed by the International Criminal Tribunal for the former Yugoslavia report that this survivor watched as Bosnian Serb soldiers pulled out other survivors from the piles of bodies, made them sing nationalist Serbian songs, and then simply put the barrels of their Kalashnikov assault rifles at the bases of their skulls and fired into their heads. Mechanical excavators were then driven into the warehouses, where they scooped up the bodies, after which the concrete floor was hosed down with water.

On July 14, at least 1,000 men and boys from Srebrenica who had spent two sweltering days without food or water in the Grbavci school buildings in the village of Orahovac were taken into nearby fields, lined up in groups of ten, and machine-gunned. One survivor peeked out from under his blindfold and saw General Ratko Mladić present at one killing session. At Branjevo Farm, between July 14 and 16, hundreds of men were shot. A participant in the killings, Dražen Erdemović, who confessed to killing at least 70 Bosnian Muslim males, was a member of the 10th Sabotage Detachment of the Bosnian Serb Army. Erdemović, who was 23 years old in 1995, was a Bosnian Croat who had joined the Bosnian Serb Army. He was an unwilling killer, an involuntary accomplice to mass murder. At first he refused to execute prisoners; he was told either do so or hand his weapon to his colleagues and join the line of men waiting to be shot. Testifying much later at The Hague,[26] he recalled that day when some 1,000 to 1,200 men were killed: "The men in front of us were ordered to turn their backs. When those men turned their backs to us, we shot at them. We were given orders to shoot."

Erdemović said that all but one of the victims wore civilian clothes and that, except for one person who tried to escape, they offered no resistance before being shot. Sometimes the executioners were particularly cruel. When some of the soldiers recognized acquaintances from Srebrenica, they beat and humiliated them before killing them. Erdemović had to persuade his fellow soldiers to stop using a belt-fed machine gun for the killings, for while it mortally wounded the prisoners, it did not cause death immediately and prolonged their suffering. Erdemović's testimony was vital because it showed that the level of willingness among the killers to complete the job was not universal. He testified that, at around 3:00 on July 16, after he and his fellow soldiers from the 10th Sabotage Detachment had finished executing the prisoners at the Branjevo Military Farm, they were told that there was a group of 500 Bosnian prisoners from Srebrenica trying to break out of a nearby Dom Kultura club. Erdemović and the other members of his unit stated flatly that they would not carry out any more executions. They were subsequently told to attend a meeting with a Bosnian Serb lieutenant colonel at a café in Pilica, and as they arrived there, they could hear the sounds of gunfire and hand grenades. The sounds lasted for approximately twenty minutes, after which a soldier from Bratunac entered the café and announced that "everything was over."[27] Later, some 20 to 30 Bosnian Serb women from Bratunac, who had been caught looting in Potočari after July 11, came in. And, somewhat underequipped with brushes, plastic buckets, and cloths, they were ordered to clean and scrub the pools of blood and mangled human remains of several hundred executed men off the club floor.[28]

Killing this number of people was no easy business, and not every Bosnian Serb soldier was willing to participate. The following coded communication was intercepted over unsecured lines[29] between VRS Main Staff Security Chief Ljubiša Beara and General Radislav Krstić, in which Beara requested assistance with disposing of the Srebrenica prisoners in the days after July 11. It becomes apparent that the two senior officers are finding it harder than expected to find men willing to carry out the daily round of mass executions:

> *Radislav Krstić (RK):* I will see what I can do, but it will disturb a lot. Please, you have
> some men down there at Nastić's and Blagojević's [*two separate VRS units*].
>
> *Ljubiša Beara (LB):* But I don't have any, and if I did—or if I did, I wouldn't still be
> asking for the third day.
>
> *RK:* Check with Blagojević, take his Red Berets [*an anti-terrorist unit with a record of
> aggressive frontline fighting*].
>
> *LB:* They're not there. Only four of them are still there. They took off, fuckers. They're
> not there anymore.

RK: I'll see what I can do.

LB: Check it out and have them go to Drago's. Krle, I don't know what to do
    anymore.

RK: Ljubo, take those MUP guys *[Interior Ministry police troops]* from up there.

LB: No, they won't do anything. I talked to them. There is no other solution but those
    15 to 30 men with Indjic.

RK: Ljubo, you have to understand me, too. You guys have fucked me up so much.

LB: I understand, but you have to understand me, too. Had this been done then, we
    wouldn't be arguing over it now.

RK: Oh, now I'll be the one to blame.

LB: I don't know what to do. I mean it, Krle, there are still 3,500 parcels that I have to
    distribute and I have no solution.

RK: I'll see what I can do.

The remains of the victims executed in surrounding villages and fields
were picked up by mechanical bulldozer and heavy earth-moving equipment and dumped into several primary mass graves. Along with them
were buried some 650 Srebrenica defenders captured over subsequent
days in surrounding oak forests and wheat fields, as well as those killed in
smaller groups at places like Tisca, by the Cerska river, on the Bratunac–
Konjević Polje road, and near Meces.

The main road from Srebrenica and Potočari runs up to the small
town of Bratunac, and it was in roughly a five- to twenty-mile radius of
these three small towns that the five main execution sites were located.
Dump trucks and buses had been busy for three days by the afternoon
of the fifteenth, ferrying the women of Srebrenica away and transporting live men and dead bodies. At the Kravica warehouses execution site,
the trucks and bulldozers drove straight inside and across the floor to
pick up the victims of the executions. These were then buried in a series
of mass graves, mainly a few miles away at Glogova. This was a huge
logistical operation: moving the thousands of terrified prisoners by bus

and truck, tying their hands with rope, telephone wire, and scraps of cloth, executing them in groups, burying them with bulldozers, and then trying to hide the evidence required massive coordination. Fuel and ammunition for executions needed to be provisioned, and officers, or their subordinates,[30] needed to sign the fuel and vehicle requisition slips.

Mladić had returned from his trip to Belgrade on July 16, irrational, irritated, and shouting orders. Time was of the essence: Mladić wanted the assaults on the nearby enclaves of Žepa and Goražde to begin, and the Bratunac and Zvornik brigades and their combat engineering capability were required for this. It was also very hot—the bodies of the dead would decompose in the summer sun. Finally, there were still prisoners to be killed and thousands of bodies to bury. So the Bosnian Serb officers had the dead men from the Kozluk bottling plant buried where they lay. The victims of Orahovac went into two pits in fields at Lazete. At Petkovici Dam and around Branjevo Farm and Pilica the men were buried on the spot. The dead from the Kravica warehouses had gone to graves at Glogova and nearby.

The Bosnian Serb soldiers were still, by July 19, engaged in operations outside Srebrenica against the remnants of the column of armed and unarmed Bosnian Muslim men from the Bosnian Army's 28th Division who had broken out of Srebrenica on the eleventh. Operations were beginning around Žepa, too. Dragan Obrenović and General Krstić were in touch with each other on July 19:

Radislav Krstić (RK): Is that you, Obrenović?

Dragan Obrenović (DO): Yes.

RK: Krstić here.

DO: How are you General, sir?

RK: I'm great, and you?

DO: Thanks to you I am too.

RK: Way to go, Chief. And how's your health?

DO: It's fine, thank God, it's fine.

RK: Are you working down there?

DO: Of course we're working.

RK: Good.

DO: We've managed to catch a few more, either by gunpoint or in mines.

RK: Kill them all. God damn it.

DO: Everything, everything is going according to plan. Yes.

RK: Not a single one must be left alive.

DO: Everything is going according to plan. Everything.

RK: Way to go, Chief. The *Turks* are probably listening to us. Let them listen, the motherfuckers.

DO: Yeah, let them.[31]

As the two were on the phone, they almost certainly didn't look up into the sky over the huge area of eastern Bosnia. But even if they had, they wouldn't have spotted the U2 reconnaissance aircraft, their cameras whirring away underneath their fuselages, flying at nearly 50,000 feet. Unknown to them, the fate of 8,000 men was being caught on camera.

Still, despite the mounting evidence of mass executions, the international community was slow to react. In some ways, it was hard for them to even conceive of murder on such a large scale. It wouldn't be long before reports started trickling out about what happened at Srebrenica. But for the moment, although everybody knew there had been a lot of violence, most people believed that the missing Muslim men had probably been imprisoned somewhere.

Chapter Three

HOW THE KILLERS TRIED TO HIDE THE EVIDENCE

Out in the summer heat of eastern Bosnia the bodies of the dead now lay where they had been dumped, in the primary mass graves.

Some 7,000 men or more had just been killed in the largest massacre in Europe since World War II, while approximately 40,000 women and children from the enclave at Srebrenica had escaped to safe territory. What happened in the weeks and months after the massacre complicated the world's greatest forensic science puzzle. The thousands of bodies from the Srebrenica killings had hardly been buried before the orders came through to dig them up again. The bodies were dug up with mechanical equipment, in the process severely breaking up or "disassociating" the remains, and were then reburied in dozens of smaller secondary mass graves, making them harder to find and identify.

Outside Srebrenica, the war continued. The enclave of Žepa fell on July 25, 1995, to Bosnian Serb troops. It left only one more pocket in eastern Bosnia, Goražde, controlled by the Bosnian government forces, and if the VRS could take this, it would leave them with clear territory all the way from Sarajevo to the Serbian border. Meanwhile, the thousands of Bosnian women and children from Srebrenica had reached Tuzla, the largest and closest town then in the territory of the Army of Bosnia and Herzegovina. Terrified, and in many cases dehydrated and suffering from heatstroke, the people displaced from Srebrenica camped out on the airfield at Eagle Airbase.

Meanwhile the tire treads of the bulldozers and dump trucks used in the killings were barely dry, and earth, grass, flowers, straw, bullet cases, and bits of human flesh were stuck in the rubber cleats of the wheels that had driven between the different massacre and burial sites.

For most of the officers and men of the Bosnian Serb forces, operations around Srebrenica in July were primarily military ones. But for some others, separate duties came up too. But after the fall of Srebrenica, logistical operations were required to transport approximately 8,000 men to their death and burial. Thus the line between military and administrative logistics was blurred when men were ordered to take part in the killings and burials and the operations surrounding them. There were Bosnian Serb officers and men who were subsequently judged by the ICTY to have been involved not just in military operations, but also in the planning and carrying out of the operation to murder the Srebrenica prisoners, bury them, and subsequently try and hide the evidence.

By the first week of August, news of the killings at Srebrenica was everywhere in Bosnia. When General Radislav Krstić visited Bosnian Serb front lines outside Zvornik on August 7, he reportedly discovered a Serb soldier listening on his transistor radio to a broadcast from Bosnian territory; it was testimony of a survivor from one of the executions three weeks earlier. When General Rupert Smith from the UN Protection Force met with Ratko Mladić in Belgrade on July 15—with Slobodan Milošević, the United Nations' Yasushi Akashi, and Carl Bildt present— Smith warned Mladić that there were "rumors" of atrocities, massacres, and rapes in Srebrenica. The presence of Mladić at the meeting should be kept secret, the participants decided,[1] because although Smith had to discuss the strategic situation in Bosnia with Mladić in his capacity as senior Bosnian Serb commander, there was a growing feeling of unease about what Mladić's men were doing in the fields of eastern Bosnia.

Also, no one wanted to highlight the close links between Mladić and Milošević, a president with whom they had to do business.

As word about the killings began to spread, information gleaned from the American U2 reconnaissance aircraft that had been flying over the three enclaves would prove vital. The pictures taken would be essential in locating the Srebrenica mass graves.

The Story of Srebrenica Emerges

The recon aircraft, code-named Dragon Lady, operated out of a British Royal Air Force base at Fairford in Gloucestershire that was often used by American Air Force heavy bombers. When it came to knowing what was going on in the Bosnian war, the American intelligence apparatus "owned the skies over Bosnia," said one British defense analyst.[2] In addition to reconnaissance, US and other NATO aircraft enforced a no-fly zone over Bosnia, and on rare occasions before mid-1995 launched airstrikes. Besides the U2s—which could fly at altitudes of up to 70,000 feet, carrying aerial cameras that could obtain very precise resolution while filming from 60,000 feet—unmanned Predator aerial vehicles also flew the recon missions. These aircraft primarily gathered information about the deployment of Serb forces and ascertained the army's readiness to launch an attack on the Muslim enclaves of Žepa and Goražde. However, in the days before and after the massacres, the footage also picked up images of the groups of men gathered on open ground near Srebrenica, as well as the large areas of disturbed earth that appeared after the men disappeared. In doing so, the aircraft unknowingly documented not just the process and aftermath of a mass killing, but the historical foundations of a revolution in forensic science, human rights, and international justice.

The Evidence of the Massacre

Only days after the massacre around Srebrenica, evidence of the crime began to mount. There were aerial photographs and testimony from survivors who had reached Tuzla after fleeing Srebrenica. Journalists and human rights officials were swift to document both. Some of the Bosnian Serb forces' rank and file knew about the executions and the burials, too. And most crucially, the international community's judicial body had already set up the ICTY to deal with war crimes in the former Yugoslavia. The truth was starting to emerge, and on July 24, the ICTY issued an indictment against Mladić for genocide, crimes against humanity, and war crimes.

Four days earlier, the first investigators had arrived in Tuzla. In a bid to highlight Mladić's responsibility, the indictment noted that the crimes in Srebrenica were committed by an army "strictly under the control from the top." The crimes were carried out with "incredible discipline, organization, and military efficiency." Serb soldiers carried out the orders, "capturing, detaining, transporting, murdering and burying" approximately 7,000 or more men and boys in just four days. According to the prosecution,[3] Ratko Mladić exercised full control over his troops at the time of the Srebrenica operation. Mladić issued orders and received regular reports about the developments in the field; he was also present in the Srebrenica and Bratunac area during the slaughter.

The victims of Srebrenica and their remains were the key pieces of evidence to the mass murders that had been committed. Thus, by August 1995, there were victims, crimes, and the alleged perpetrators. What needed to follow were justice, retribution, and reconciliation. But before forensic experts arrived to start looking for the dead, other investigators began looking for the living—the perpetrators at large in Bosnia, Serbia, and elsewhere.

In 1993 United Nations Security Council Resolution 827 had established the ICTY after a UN commission of experts had determined in a report in 1992 that grave breaches of international humanitarian law and of the Geneva Conventions had taken place in the former Yugoslavia since 1991. It was the first international war crimes court established since the Nuremberg and Tokyo tribunals in 1945, and its mandate was clear: to investigate and prosecute war crimes that took place in the former Yugoslavia from 1991 onward. The ICTY could try individual persons—not organizations, political parties, army units, administrative entities, or other legal subjects—for grave breaches of the 1949 Geneva Conventions, violations of the laws or customs of war, genocide, and crimes against humanity.[4]

The tribunal was also established to be judicially and operationally pursuant to the legal doctrine known as "clean hands," whereby "he who seeks equity does so equitably." This means that the court had to behave in complete adherence to international law in its cases against alleged war criminals. The killers from Srebrenica may have behaved in a lawless manner, but the judicial process to bring them to account, and those implementing it, had to be in accordance with the law in the measured justice of prosecution and defense.

This had not been the case at the trials at the International Military Tribunal at Nuremberg that began in 1945. The Allies, specifically the Russians, had been in breach of the doctrine that specified that no state may accuse another state of violations of international law and exercise criminal jurisdiction over the latter's citizens in respect of such violations if it is itself guilty of similar violations. The defense in the trials of German officers argued that "the Tribunal could not legitimately convict the defendants of the crime of aggression when the Soviet Union, which cooperated in the establishment of the Military Tribunal, had also engaged in a war of aggression in complicity with Germany." In the "High Command Case,"[5] the Military Tribunal ruled that "under general principles of law, an accused does not exculpate himself from a crime by showing that another committed a similar crime, either before or after the alleged commission of the crime by the accused."

The "clean hands" doctrine meant not only that the cases against Ratko Mladić and those accused of similar crimes had to be prepared, executed, prosecuted, defended, and judged in the most legally scrupulous manner, but that it had to be shown that whoever established the tribunal could not be accused of complicity in crimes similar to those it was trying.

The tribunal was housed and headquartered in a former insurance company's 1960s building in the Dutch capital, The Hague; its detention center was two miles away on the North Sea coast at Scheveningen, where detainees awaiting trial, and those on trial, were housed in a specially constructed prison building that had been purpose-built for the ICTY. By 1994 more than 200 staff were employed, and the first field investigations began: the first indictment was issued in 1994 against Dragan Nikolić, a Bosnian Serb concentration camp commander. In March 1994 the subject of the tribunal's first trial, Duško Tadić, was arrested by German police in Munich on a warrant issued on charges of atrocities committed while involved with the workings of the Keraterm, Omarska, and Trnopolje concentration camps in northern Bosnia. These had been run by Serbs and had included as detainees Muslim and in some cases Croat civilians from the area around the town of Prijedor in northwestern Bosnia. By June 1996, 68 indictments had been confirmed against 101 individuals. The international community was clearly willing to bring war criminals from the former Yugoslavia to justice.

But judicial machinations in The Hague and political will in other international capitals moved slowly. In the meantime, the perpetrators of the Srebrenica killings went back to the scene of their crimes, dug up the thousands of victims, and reburied them in an attempt to cover their tracks.

Where the Bodies Were Buried

There were five very large primary burial sites of the victims, each site containing one or more actual graves.[6] These were at the Petkovici Dam, at the Kozluk bottling plant, at Orahovac, and at Branjevo Military Farm near Pilica, while the bodies from the Kravica agricultural cooperative warehouses were buried jointly at Glogova and Radnice, which consisted of at least four primary graves. The first part of the Serbian operation to hide the evidence was to seal the primary burial sites from outside observation and interference. This was done at all of the areas, especially the Glogova sites, since they lay near roads.

Dump trucks and bulldozers with front and back scoops were used. The first thing that the operation accomplished was the massive and instantaneous breaking up of the buried bodies, which were in various stages of decomposition, with burial times averaging around eight weeks in hot summer conditions. The sight and smell would have been appalling. Decomposition was such that the appendages detached from bodies, but clothing tended to keep torsos and legs together, if the mechanical diggers did not break them up. Tissue and organ decay varied greatly depending on soil conditions. Moving and exposing remains to the oxygen in the air accelerated the decomposition in the secondary graves.

To undertake this horrific act, the logistical considerations, such as providing fuel for the diggers and the availability of trucks, were considerable. But all these activities were planned, implemented, and signed off on. The brutality of the decision to dig up the remains of several thousand human beings can be better appreciated if one reduces the operation to a simple mathematical calculation. Begin with the very rough assumption that each decomposing body weighed about 50 kilograms when killed, taking into consideration the poor diet inside the enclave, which potentially lowers the estimate. The body weight would then have been reduced by between 50 to 75 percent from putrefaction by the time the bodies were dug up, some of the body mass reduced due to decomposing fluids that drained into the surrounding earth. So, taking each composite body mass at roughly just over twelve kilograms, approximately 100,000 kilograms of dead people needed to be moved. This would have required around 50 truckloads at two tons of decomposing human per truck, including the often substantial extra weight of rocks, earth, clothing, and assorted detritus from the respective graves. This means there was approximately 3.2 tons of this putrefactive mixture in each of the 29 to 31 secondary burial sites. The graves varied in size, but the parts of between 40 to 320 people were pushed into the secondary mass graves.

Regardless of the mathematical variations, it was an enormous undertaking. Witnesses living in Bratunac described the "incredible stench" of the lorries passing through the streets in the summer night, and some children reported finding, the morning after, some legs that had fallen off the trucks during the night as they passed through the town.[7]

The bodies also carried evidence with them. The Vitinka bottling plant in Kozluk, a small town near Zvornik, puts carbonated mineral water into distinctive green glass containers, with white labels that include green leaves surrounded by red lettering. Srebrenica men had been executed on the garbage dump at the Vitinka bottling plant, and when their bodies were moved, broken green glass and Vitinka labels were moved as well, leaving a trail from the primary to the secondary burial site. Along a narrow asphalt track that turns off the main road to Zvornik is the Čančari Road. At least twelve secondary mass grave sites were dug here, and scraps of green glass from Vitinka were easily visible in at least one.

The stones, flowers, Kalashnikov cartridge cases, and grass from the primary mass grave at Orahovac were, along with hundreds of dismembered bodies, transported to seven hidden graves near Hodžići; the earth in the new graves told its own story of where it had actually come from.

These are just two examples of the crisscrossed forensic archaeological clues that investigators had to look at. Clues that came from the five primary burial sites, as well as the around 30 "secondary" burial sites, were spread over some 300 square miles of land. Within this space were hidden and buried vast quantities of the approximately 1,668,000 bones and pieces of body, commingled, mixed up, that had made up the estimated 8,100 human beings who were reported and estimated missing in the months and years following the fall of the Srebrenica enclave. One man's remains were later found in four separate mass graves miles apart. The thousands of remains were now buried in pits in lost valleys, beside remote roads, and in clearings and on the edges of forests and woods. The killers, the perpetrators, the planners, and those who had buried the bodies thought they had got away with murder.

NATO Airstrikes, the End of War, and Its Aftermath

NATO's Operation Deliberate Force, which involved airstrikes and artillery fire on Bosnian Serb positions in the Republika Srpska and around Sarajevo, began on August 30, 1995. Mladić, to escape being hit by any incoming bombs or missiles, had moved to his headquarters outside Han Pijesak in eastern Republika Srpska, near the road between Sokolac and Vlasenica. On September 10, a Bosnian army post intercepted this transmission from General Momir Talic of the Krajina Corps, fighting a losing battle in western Bosnia, to Mladić: "We have lost, if you do not instruct 'The Hairy One' [Karadžić] to stop this war on a political level, then we are done for."

On the same day, the commander of UN forces in former Yugoslavia, French lieutenant general Bernard Janvier, met with Mladić, who'd returned to Belgrade, accompanied by Yugoslav foreign minister Milan Milutinovic and Bosnian Serb vice president Nikola Koljevic. The only subject on the agenda was forthcoming peace talks. The end was in sight for the Serbs. Four days later, on September 14, General Smith's headquarters in Sarajevo received a faxed letter from Mladić's headquarters in Han Pijesak about discussing the conditions of the pull-back of Serb artillery around Sarajevo.

But before the war ended, before peace talks took place, and before Mladić disappeared, he reputedly tried to make one rather desperate last-ditch attempt at removing the indictment from the ICTY that he privately thought dogged his substantial and formidable reputation as a military commander. He attempted this through a technique he had mastered since the beginning of the war when dealing with the international community: hostage taking. Two French aircrew personally experienced Ratko Mladić post-Srebrenica and were among the very few international personnel to see him after July 1995. Their story gives an excellent insight into what Mladić was doing at this late stage of the war, where he was, and how the Serb government apparatus in Belgrade viewed his position and behavior following the massacre at Srebrenica.

Serb forces had shot down a French Mirage jet on August 30. Its crew, Captain Frederic Chiffot and Lieutenant Jose Souvignet, ejected and, on hitting the ground outside Pale, were instantly surrounded by a Serb patrol. One of them broke his ankle on landing; both were beaten by their captors, with Captain Chiffot suffering a broken nose. They were filmed alive with their Bosnian Serb captors shortly thereafter on the same day.

Soon after their capture, Mladić himself interrogated the two downed French airmen. According to the airmen's later accounts, he reportedly told them that they would have to watch each other being tortured and that they would be executed. A Serb hospital employee deliberately struck Captain Chiffot's broken nose and knocked him unconscious several times. The two men were locked up in a bunker and held in solitary confinement for much of the time. "About every three days, a guard threw us some food," the men were quoted as saying in a newspaper report published by the French newspaper *Le Canard Enchaine*.[8] The account also said that the Serbs staged mock executions and strangling, and also kicked their wounded legs several times. This information came out only eventually after their release: in fear of antagonizing the Serb leadership, and by extension Serbian president Slobodan Milošević, as well as jeopardizing the about-to-be-signed Dayton Peace Accords, a senior French military officer reportedly instructed the two pilots to say that they had been treated according to the Geneva Conventions.

Serbian president Slobodan Milošević, Croatian president Franjo Tuđman, and Bosnian president Alija Izetbegović, under the eyes of the international community, hammered out the Dayton Peace Accords at an Ohio airbase. By February 1996 the peace deal, which also included a blueprint for what a future constitution of Bosnia might look like, had been signed and ratified in Paris. Bosnia was split into two: the Muslim-Croat Federation, with its capital in Sarajevo, and the Serb-dominated horseshoe of land that stretched around the north and east of the country, called the Republika Srpska. In the words of the veteran British television journalist Ed Vulliamy, who had discovered the Bosnian Serb–run concentration camp at Omarska, "rarely has mass murder been so amply rewarded at the negotiating table."[9]

Within the Republika Srpska, with its capital in the northern town of Banja Luka, thousands of demobilized former members of the Bosnian Serb Army, including many who had operated at Srebrenica, lived and circulated freely, like their senior commander. Despite having been indicted for genocide, war crimes, and crimes against humanity in 1995 by the ICTY, General Mladić was still a serving soldier living in plain sight in eastern Bosnia. In 1996, the war over, he moved around eastern Bosnia under the very eyes of some of the 54,000 NATO peacekeepers of the NATO Implementation Force (IFOR), code-named Operation Joint Endeavour, deployed into Bosnia from December 1995 to December 1996 to keep the former warring sides apart and carry out the military annexes of the Dayton Accords. These accords had three major goals: ending hostilities, authorizing a structured military and civilian program, and establishing a central Bosnian government while excluding individuals that served sentences or were under indictment by international war crimes tribunals.

For NATO, particularly the Americans, force protection, or the security of their troops, was of paramount importance. For the first year of the peacekeepers' time in Bosnia, arresting war criminals at large in Bosnia was not in NATO's mandate, unless the soldiers were to come across them in the normal course of their duties. Keeping the warring parties apart and maintaining the Dayton Accords was the order of the day. For now, NATO and the West had a hands-off approach when it came to arresting war criminals.

In this climate, it is easy to see how wanted war criminals could move around freely. In the immediate aftermath of the war, Mladić lived in his former military barracks near Han Pijesak, well within the Republika Srpska. Mladić made sure he was nowhere in sight when NATO weapons inspection teams, mandated to observe the disarmament of the various armies in post-war Bosnia, visited the barracks in 1996 and 1997. Shortly, though, at the end of 1997, Mladić moved eastward, across the Drina into Serbia, to accept the more receptive hospitality of the military there, away from a country controlled by NATO soldiers who, without warning, could reverse their operational procedures and decide to arrest him.

Taking all of this into account, in autumn 1997, the Republika Srpska was not a welcoming place for an international forensic or judicial investigator digging for evidence of the crimes that had been committed only two years before. The alleged perpetrators and their subordinates were still circulating freely. The cautious, conservative estimate of those at liberty inside Bosnia—Muslim, Croat, or Serb—who had committed crimes or war crimes, directly or indirectly, was estimated to be in the low thousands. And the perpetrators and their victims were in many cases going to end up living side by side. The only way that this situation could ever be redressed, the only way that reconciliation could be retribution instead of revenge would be through the implementation of justice.

NATO did not want to risk destabilizing the very fragile peace between Serbs, Muslims, and Croats. Arresting Serb and Croat war criminals could destabilize an extremely delicate status quo. Radovan Karadžić even went so far as to say over the air on Serb television in 1996 that NATO was treating any Serb who had carried a weapon in the war as a potential arrest target. If any members of their leadership were arrested, each Bosnian Serb was to take it as a personal attack and to respond accordingly.

It was also proving very difficult, up until mid-1997, to achieve a "coalition of the willing" among the French, the Americans, and the British over what action to take on arresting war criminals. In the aftermath of the signing of the Dayton Peace Accords in Paris in 1996, US president Clinton and his French counterpart Jacques Chirac tried to find common ground. Chirac was outraged that the two French Mirage fighter pilots had been badly beaten and personally threatened by Mladić while in captivity. Substantial and substantive reports, too, had now appeared about what had happened at Srebrenica. Clinton was cut between the imperatives of US troop force protection and the need to see justice done. He needed heavy encouragement from other NATO partners, but initially the British were reluctant to act. Arrest operations of war criminals could trigger reprisals against NATO forces and see the peace deal fail.

Britain's soldiers had fought valiantly and hard in Bosnia—against the Croats in particular—protecting humanitarian convoys, laying down an operational line in the sand, and showing all sides that they would stretch the restrictive UNPROFOR mandate's tiniest sub-clause if it justified opening fire on the enemy. The rampaging, ethnically cleansing Croat paramilitary and military units in central Bosnia learned this quickly and painfully.

The British also acted as observers in the enclaves like Goražde and around Sarajevo itself. The British military was relatively good at dealing with the brutal and deceptive absolutism of the Balkans war-fighting mindset. They were former colonial warriors—flexible and empirical—and they had experience not just with terrorism in places like Northern Ireland but with the so-called "bush-fire wars" that had accompanied the breakup of their former colonies. However, in Bosnia they were on a quasi-peacekeeping mission in the middle of a war, and their main job was to protect the supply of humanitarian aid, not to engage with the various combatant factions. Although they had spent decades fighting the Cold War, they had never had to deal face-to-face with an enemy like the Serbs and Croats, who did not play by the rules of traditional enemies. But they were fast to adapt and react and, despite the limitations of their mandate, used every opportunity to confront those who held up supplies of humanitarian aid, profited from the war, or abused the civilian population. In central Bosnia, for instance, in 1992–1993, marauding Bosnian Croat paramilitary and irregular units learned that opening fire on the British Cheshire Regiment brought a tough and uncompromising response in the form of 30 mm cannon fire from the British Warrior armored vehicles.

Bosnia demanded more of foreign peacekeepers than just the ability to win the upper hand in civil-military operations like those in 1992 and 1993. Strategically flexible and militarily imaginative leaders like British general Rupert Smith understood this and realized what American Air Force generals had been saying all along: the Serbs only understood force. To them, negotiation and compromise were gray areas to be scorned at every opportunity. This was a key difference between the Serbs and the more militarily adept NATO forces. An apt summary was to be made by an Albanian rebel fighter in the Kosovo Liberation Army in summer 1999, after watching troops from the US 82nd Airborne Division and the British Parachute Regiment enter Kosovo: "Here in the Balkans, we

Albanians and Serbs, we understand violence. You Brits, you understand fighting."[10]

However, the capable and muscular British military were let down by their political leaders. The British Conservative administration of Prime Minister Major with Foreign Secretary Douglas Hurd had backed the UN arms embargo put in place by a UN Security Council resolution against the former Yugoslavia in September 1991. Since Bosnian Serbs had inherited the majority of the Yugoslav National Army's arsenal and the Croats could ship weapons in via their coast, the embargo hurt the Bosnian Muslims the most. Supporting it was a posture heavily criticized, particularly by the Americans and by some NATO, UN, and European Union partners, and, naturally, by the Muslims themselves. The policy of the British government of Prime Minister John Major and Foreign Secretary Douglas Hurd seemed to many to take a line of appeasement and to fall for the repeated, hollow assurances of the Serbian leaders. Allegations that full responsibility for NATO's failure to act militarily lay in London's parliamentary corridors were perhaps excessively harsh: other major actors were also involved, including the Germans, the French, the Italians, NATO, the UN, and the EU. Outside NATO, enormous culpability lay with the UN-approved mandate for the deployment of the multinational Protection Force in Bosnia, which effectively declawed some of the more effective military units.

Although historical hindsight is easy, Europe and the United States were taken by surprise on too many occasions by what happened in Bosnia. Too few people in the UN, the EU, and NATO saw what needed to happen until it was too late, and the ones who had workable solutions to the problem had neither the power nor the assets. But whereas the governmental representatives of the United Kingdom (and occasionally other nations) tended to fall for the hollow assurances of the Serbs, the more pragmatic Americans largely did not.

Foreign military and humanitarian personnel arriving and working in Bosnia were often surprised and appalled, at all stages of the war, at how badly all sides could behave toward each other. They were also astonished at the corrupt and selfish behavior of so many of the local political leaders, something large segments of the population seemed prepared to tolerate. But despite the international community's operational habit of delivering repeated lectures to the Bosnian population on good, democratic behavior, it had to be remembered, said many Bosnians, that countries like Germany, the United Kingdom, America, and France had only finished fighting a world war in 1945, fifty years before. Sometimes the local population felt it was a touch premature to be on the receiving end of international lectures on best democratic practice.

In September 1996, the first general elections for the country's tri-ethnic, three-person rotating presidency were held since the war, and 2.5 million votes were cast. Many said this election was wildly premature, and that attention should be focused on rebuilding the country's infrastructure, particularly the key areas of healthcare, education, and the rule of law. Naturally, most Serbs voted for Bosnian Serb Momčilo Krajišnik, who won the election. (He was later found guilty of crimes against humanity by the ICTY.)

By 1997 a fragile peace had been in place for two years. And as international justice was pursued and a human rights–based approach to dealing with missing persons began to take root, something was happening—or, more importantly, not happening—in Bosnia that made all of the political infighting look petty and vain and obsolete. Somehow, in the developmental apocalypse of post-war Bosnia, there was no mass vengeance, no incidents of Bosnian Muslims, for example, taking large-scale revenge on Serbs.

Why? Had the reconciliatory ideals of justice and dealing with problems like missing persons borne unexpectedly positive results so soon?

Were all sides so tired of and traumatized by war that they had no interest in repeating it? Or were those in positions of power simply focusing on cementing their political security and concentrating on making as much money, legal and illegal, as possible? External forces had halted the war just as the Serbs were losing, the Croats were eleven miles or so from Banja Luka, and NATO airstrikes had lifted the siege of Sarajevo. If this progress against the Serbs had been allowed to continue, instead of rewarding them, as some said, with the recognized establishment of the Republika Srpska, land they had taken by force, then Bosnia would have been equally divided. But it wasn't. All three sides lived in separate ethnic fiefdoms.

Sir Jeremy Greenstock, Britain's former special envoy to Iraq in the aftermath of the coalition occupation in 2003, said that jobs were the absolute key to preventing a divided country from becoming rife with sectarianism. His assessment of Iraq could be applied to Bosnia as well, although we might add the word "security" to that calculation. Both countries had enormous problems with missing persons—in the former Yugoslavia, the number of people who had gone missing in a decade of conflict was estimated to be around 40,000. In Iraq a very conservative estimate was of some 350,000 people missing from two Gulf Wars, the regime of Saddam Hussein, the insurgency, and the Iran–Iraq war of the 1980s. Both Bosnia and Iraq had thousands of foreign troops deployed in the aftermath of the conflicts. The economy in both countries was moribund. But Bosnia had not dissolved into sectarian, quasi–civil war like that racking Iraq two years after the Coalition Provisional Authority arrived in 2003. In Bosnia the popular explanation was that it was better to have somebody of your own ethnicity in power, regardless of how badly they had behaved during the war. And in this arena of zero-sum political economics just a few years after the war, tolerance, if not reconciliation, seemed to be taking hold. There was not total peace, but there was a glaring absence of war. The presence of thousands of armed NATO peacekeepers with armored vehicles, helicopters, and massive firepower certainly contributed to this. And while there are a variety of complex reasons for this, two of them were important factors in Bosnia: justice was starting to be administered, as was resolution for the thousands whose relatives were missing. And the two were inextricably interlinked.

Chapter Four

DIGGING UP THE EVIDENCE OF MASS MURDER

B osnia had to start dealing with the concurrent problems of justice and missing persons in fairly short order after the war, and these two issues were connected in ways that helped stave off violent repri-sals in the newly designated territories. Two things contributed to this perhaps surprising post-war stability: first, the international commu-nity started dealing with things fairly quickly. The ICTY had started to indict war criminals before their victims were long buried: The Hague Tribunal indicted Ratko Mladić a *week* after he committed the crimes he is alleged to have orchestrated. The foreigners, as Bosnians liked to call them, put huge pressure on the inhabitants of the country to adhere to the Dayton Peace Accords. Second, because of the workable peace that existed in the country so quickly after the war, it was easier to quickly exhume the corpses from the mass graves. Implementing justice and hu-man rights absolutism is almost impossible to do while triggers are still being pulled. The Office of the High Representative and international diplomats advised the new Bosnian government in Sarajevo and Banja Luka that dealing with the problem of missing persons was a priority—a painful and certainly protracted one, but a priority.

Compare this to Iraq after 2003, where the missing persons prob-lem was impossible to deal with until five years after the conflict ended because of the total lack of security, and because the Iraqi government didn't make a formal request for help from outsiders until then. The US-led Office for Regime Crimes started exhuming some sites immediately after the conflict to provide evidence in the trial against Saddam Hussein and his acolytes, but the implementation of substantial mechanisms to help deal with the missing persons issue took more time.

So, shortly after the end of the war, in the summer of 1997, British archaeologist Ian Hanson and a forensic team from the ICTY arrived in Bosnia. Hanson had been excavating medieval monasteries and prehistoric landscapes in London ahead of building and urban development around the dock area in the city's East End and was personally asked by the ICTY to help with the forensic excavations in Bosnia.[1] The team began work outside the northeastern Bosnian town of Brčko: perpetrators had blown up Brčko's mosque and dumped parts of it into mass graves in an attempt to hide the bodies of war crimes victims. These graves contained the Bosnian Muslim and Croat victims of Bosnian Serb ethnic cleansing of eastern Bosnia in 1992 and 1993. But with winter approaching, the all-too-short "digging season," as it became known among the forensic teams operating in Bosnia, closed. Snow was on its way, and the ground was starting to freeze. The team had made some limited progress, but the real task lay ahead of them, because there were estimated to be dozens of mass graves across Bosnia, and nobody knew quite how big some of them were going to be.

Hanson came back in 1998 to excavate the Srebrenica mass graves. This team was led by Richard Wright, Professor Emeritus of Anthropology from Sydney University. Together with Jon Sterenberg, who had a background in the British Army and was one of Australia's leading archaeologists, an archaeological photographer, and Hanson, the group formed one of the core teams to investigate sites. They began their work at the Petkovici Dam site, about 26 miles from Srebrenica, where aerial photos from the U2s confirmed that the rock and earth on the level base of the dam's revetment had been disturbed, and that it had been disturbed yet again between September 7 and 27, 1995. When he and the team first examined the site in 1998, Hanson observed shell cases from automatic weapons and fragments of skull lying strewn across the dam plateau, potential evidence of the executions. When the grave was initially opened by Wright's team, many bodies appeared to have disappeared. Still, bones, body parts, clothing, and evidence of extensive decay remained. Mechanical apparatus had obviously been used, confirmed by tire tracks, which had considerably disturbed the contents of the grave. Wright discovered the partial remains of no more than 43 persons.

Aerial imagery indicated the human remains had been moved elsewhere and reburied in secondary graves, many of which were located during the 1998 investigations. One such grave, created prior to October 2, 1995, was called "Liplje 2." The graves at Liplje lay in terrain between Zvornik and the previously mentioned sites at Čančari Road. In Liplje 2 the broken and disarticulated remains of at least 191 individuals were unearthed. One remarkable discovery at Liplje 2 was pages from Dutch newspapers, which were also found at three other burial sites. These newspapers originated with the Dutch UN peacekeepers who had so notably failed to defend the Srebrenica enclave. It was yet another link with the men who had been transported from Srebrenica.

When Hanson first got to the Petkovici Dam, investigators thought the grave had not yet been disturbed by Bosnian Serb perpetrators trying to cover their tracks. He and his colleagues mapped the skull fragments and shell cases on the surface. When they started digging, they found the first of many Seiko 5 Day-Date digital watches, popular in those days. When the wearer moved his or her arm or hand, the watch wound itself automatically. When the wearer's arm stopped moving, the watch would stop working within 24 to 36 hours. The watch that the team found in this grave showed the date of Sunday the sixteenth.[2] There were two months in 1995 where the sixteenth fell on a Sunday: April and July. And the grave had definitely been dug after April. If the watch had stopped in July, it had wound down to a halt a day after the wearer was supposed to have been executed. It didn't look like a coincidence.

Meanwhile, Srebrenica was deep inside the Republika Srpska and controlled by Bosnian Serbs, making it sometimes hard for Hanson and other Hague investigatory and forensic teams to work properly, as they were under the constant eye of local authorities not pleased at their presence there. One day one of the investigating team reported seeing photographs of all their team members stuck up on a wall in the local Republika Srpska police station. Soldiers from NATO were assigned to guard them and the sites they were working on. One of these detachments, remembers Hanson, was a clued-up and independent-minded team of American Navy SEALs who seemed to approve of the work the ICTY men and women were doing, and so were happy to look after them out in the badlands of the Republika Srpska.

As we've seen, the perpetrators exhumed and moved the evidence, and assumed they had gotten away with murder. The police forensic side of the investigation, as opposed to the archaeological one, was led by Jean-René Ruez, a 37-year-old French senior investigator for the ICTY. His training as a former police commissioner in Nice had prepared him for what he would later call "the incredible fun of chasing criminals."[3] He began his investigation in Tuzla on July 20, 1995, days after the massacre at Srebrenica had taken place. Other members of the investigating, judicial, and forensic team dealing with Srebrenica included Bill Haglund, a forensic anthropologist from Washington state who had dealt with mass burial exhumations in such places as Rwanda and Guatemala. He worked as the United Nations' senior forensic advisor for the international criminal tribunals for both Rwanda and the former Yugoslavia.[4] He led the forensic team in 1996. Australian Richard Wright, originally from Bristol in England, but long settled in Sydney, took over leading the forensic team in July 1997. It was Wright's pioneering application of pure archaeology that would enable them and others to start piecing together the hundreds of thousands of forensic clues that they pulled out of the ground around Srebrenica.

Professor Wright had previously worked on an exhumation in the Ukraine of Holocaust victims executed in World War II by a German SS Einsatzkommando with local Ukrainian help. If archaeology can be said to be, in the words of Ian Hanson, "the applied science of reconstructing human history and behavior from physical remains,"[5] then dating the various actions that constitute this behavior is of paramount importance. In the Ukraine, Wright's team found the shell cases from German Lugers and Walter P-38 pistols in a grave. Stamped on the bottom of these cartridge cases were the date and place of manufacture in Germany. The latest date on the cases was 1941, which provided a *terminus post quem*, meaning that the killings could not have taken place before then. To establish the *terminus ante quem*, or latest date that the killings could have happened, the team used radiocarbon assays to date the hair that was still attached to some of the corpses, particularly the female ones, many of whom had their long hair braided in Ukrainian-style plaits. This provided evidence that the events had taken place between the years 1941 and 1952. The experience Wright brought to the Srebrenica investigation was important—he would apply the same careful detective work he had used in the Ukraine.

When the investigators and forensic experts from the ICTY arrived at the Srebrenica sites in April 1998, there was no shortage of evidence on the surface of the sites themselves. The Hague team under Jean-René Ruez set about exhuming the sites, one of the first of which was the Petkovici Dam primary burial site. Metal detector sweeps of the surface area had found hundreds of cartridge cases lying among the rocks and in the scruffy brown and yellow sunburnt grass. There was a pattern to the cases, lying in a rough straight line: opposite them were scattered the hundreds of cranial and other bone fragments. When fired, Kalashnikov rifles expel spent cartridges via the ejection port on the right-hand side of the weapon, which climb and spin at a diagonal in clockwise turns, before landing approximately four to six feet forward of the shooter's right shoulder.[6] The investigating team at the Petkovici Dam could thus place the rough whereabouts of the line of executioners from the so-called "distribution map" of the hundreds of Kalashnikov cases scattered around.

When a 7.62 mm lead bullet with a copper coating, traveling at 715 meters per second, enters the frontal plates of the human cranium, it forces the cranium backward against the supporting strength of the spine in a whiplash effect, akin to the victims' head nodding almost at the speed of sound. The bullet immediately decelerates inside the skull after encountering the shock resistance of the frontal cranial bone. This causes the bullet to "tumble," or rotate, tearing through the brain tissue before exiting the skull. The entrance wound can often be little larger than the diameter of the bullet itself, but the exit wound can be the size of a baby's fist.[7] The rear cranial plate is fractured and fragmented, and the air vacuum that travels immediately behind the bullet blows the pieces of the skull back and outward from the head at extremely high speed in a whirling conglomeration. It is not uncommon for persons standing in the immediate vicinity of somebody shot in the head to be hit by pieces of skull fragment. So when hundreds of men are shot in the head and body at close range by Kalashnikov assault rifles, the back spray of detaching cranial fragments will form a pattern, indicating where the executed victims were standing.

So for Richard Wright, Ian Hanson, and the rest of the team standing that spring on the Petkovici Dam, the bullet cases and skull fragments gave them a good idea of where the killers and their victims had stood. They'd marked the cranial fragments with orange flags, to show where the victims had fallen, and they'd examined the spread of the cartridge cases, and thus had their execution lines. With the assistance of the aerial photos taken by the U2 aircraft on hand, they began to excavate the site. As the Caterpillar quarrying machine, or "Rubber Duck," started to remove rocks from the grave, it quickly became apparent that somebody had been there already. Different colored and textured soils from a variety of depths were mixed in with the first layer of earth extracted, meaning a large hole—in this case, a grave—had existed, but had been filled in. Not sure what they would find there, the team excavated the entire grave and found a variety of human body parts, mostly in stages four and five of decomposition, that comprised 43 bodies.

The Science of Taphonomy

There are five main stages to the process of human decomposition, and Ian Hanson had seen all five during his time as an archaeologist. These included the bodies of civilians murdered by the army on a lakeside in Guatemala; Congolese soldiers exhumed from under a garden in Kisangani on the Congo River; the desiccated and partly mummified remains, thousands of years old, found at a pyramid complex in Egypt; the windblown, well-preserved corpses of Iraqis and Kurdish civilians killed by soldiers loyal to Saddam Hussein; and the thousands of corpses of the Srebrenica victims. The science of taphonomy, or what happens to organisms during and after decomposition, was a grimly familiar one. The five stages of this can be summarized as the acronym FBAAD. This stands for Fresh, Bloat, Active, Advanced, and Dry. Stage one, or fresh decomposition, occurs when the body has been dead for a few hours, its blood coalescing in its veins and muscles after the heart has stopped beating. A hanged man, for instance, will appear to have unnaturally dark blue or black extremities where the blood has gathered. A process called autolysis takes place, whereby the immediate decay in the body causes a release of cellular enzymes into the body's cells and muscular tissue, which begin the process of decomposition. The existing oxygen in the corpse disappears, and anaerobic organisms from the throat, lungs, stomach, and intestines begin to turn the proteins and lipids—molecules that contain fats, vitamins, and waxes—of the actual muscular and organic structure of the body (its flesh and organs) into acids and gases, like methane and hydrogen sulphide.

In stage two, these gases then fill and bloat the body. By stage three, active decay, maggots move on to the body, and almost all of the liquids in it are purged outward as the tissues in the corpse break down and liquefy. By stage four, advanced decay, most of the body's material has broken down, having decomposed and liquefied into the surrounding earth, forming a heavily stained and marked area around the body known as a "corpse decomposition island." The ground in this area will now contain more carbon and nitrogen, as well as calcium, phosphorus, and magnesium. These materials are responsible for the increased rate of plant growth in areas where bodies are buried. By stage five, the body's remains are dry and almost skeletonized.

The science of human decomposition, meanwhile, is something that forensic scientists not just at the ICMP but in crime laboratories, mortuaries, and in the main world centers of academia had learned much about by the end of the twentieth century. The exhumed bodies of the Srebrenica victims were in varied states of decomposition when they were taken out of the ground by the forensic investigators. In the heavy, wet clay and acidic black earth of the mountains and forests of eastern Bosnia, human tissue disintegration sets in reasonably quickly. Temperature, the amount of oxygen, the amount of moisture in the soil, and the soil's pH balance, or respective acidity and alkalinity, are just four factors that can accelerate or slow down the process of decomposition in a mass grave. In a number of the secondary mass graves the bodies and body parts were so tightly mingled and packed, literally glued together by decaying tissue, that almost no oxygen had reached them, resulting in some preservation of some of the bodies.

The process of decomposition normally advances to a point where saponification—literally, "turning to soap"—takes place, whereby the resultant soft tissue in any conversion of the body fat and fatty acids of a corpse is turned into adipocere, a substance most commonly called "grave wax." The derivation of the word is from the Latin *adeps*, meaning "fat or fleshy, or pertaining to fat," and *cera,* meaning "wax." This process is more common where the amount of fatty tissues in the body is high, agents of decomposition are absent or only minutely present, and the burial ground is particularly damp. This grave wax, which stinks, is a brownish-white adhesive gloop of decomposing tissue that falls off the skeletal structure fairly quickly. (The two parts of a human corpse that last longest are its bones—particularly teeth and long bones such as tibias and femurs—and clothing. When it comes to garments, Levi's clothing, on statistical evidence, is among that which often seems to last longest and best.[8])

But sometimes human remains do not last very long at all. Hanson remembers an excavation looking for bodies of civilians killed by the army in Guatemala and then buried by a lake. There was nothing left of them: all Hanson and his colleagues could find was a few straw sombreros, scraps of clothing, and some coffin nails. The bodies had totally, utterly disappeared, dissolved by soil acidity, bacteria, and seasonal fluctuations of the lake dissolving and flushing the organic material away. "It was hard to try and take a DNA sample from a fragment of bone where the skeleton had dissolved," Hanson had said. "The Guatemalans thought it was witchcraft, that spirits had stolen the body."

The forensic evidence of hundreds of cartridge cases and cranial fragments certainly suggested the execution at the Petkovici Dam. Other forensic pointers at other secondary grave sites, such as cloth and wire ligatures used to tie the wrists, also indicated large-scale executions. There were blindfolds used to cover eyes, some with bullet holes through them. And more Seiko 5 Day-Date watches were found. Coincidentally,

Richard Wright was a collector of automatic watches and recognized the evidential power of these artifacts, as they literally pinpointed time of death. Dozens of watches were recovered from the graves over the years. Out of ten watches found in 1998, eight showed the day and date of Saturday the fifteenth or Sunday the sixteenth. The probability that all the watches randomly stopped on these dates was trillions to one. This was no coincidence.

But there were simply not enough bodies at the dam site to correlate the size of the reported execution, the surface evidence, and the contents of the mass burial pit. It was clear to the team that most of the bodies had been removed. This theory held up later when they dug up a grave in a field some twenty meters from a narrow asphalted access track that led to the village of Čančari. The broken-up bodies had clearly not originated at this location but had been brought from elsewhere, a finding backed by the evaluation of soils foreign to the location. The man operating the mechanical backhoe for the team uncovered a green bottle fragment in the soil, which was initially thought to have been broken upon its removal from the ground. However, the Vitinka label on the glass suggested it came from the company's bottling plant near the town of Kozluk. Richard Wright immediately suspected that there could be a primary mass grave site near this village. When the team of fifteen archaeologists and anthropologists, US and Dutch crime scene officers, and Russian troops attached to the NATO mission traveled there, they found the evidence they suspected. There was a rubbish pit next to the Drina River behind the bottling factory with open holes in the ground and labels and bits of green glass everywhere. Two human legs were lying in the rubbish. Evidence excavated at this site in 1999–2000 showed that several hundred men had been shot there on the slope of broken green glass.

From what they found at Petkovici, Čančari, and Kozluk, the investigators could deduce only one thing, which Mladić and his co-conspirators already knew: the primary graves had all been robbed. The men from The Hague suddenly realized that they were now not simply dealing with two or three mass graves, each dug in the absolute immediate vicinity of the five or six main execution sites, but there was also a very real possibility that for each primary site, four, five, six, or more secondary burial sites could also exist. The investigation team realized that the bodies of the thousands of victims were likely to be buried in dozens of relocated graves across the wild surrounding countryside, some of which could prove impossible to find.

Exhuming the Bodies

Before removing the remains of each of the 43 bodies they had found in the first grave, the investigators first surveyed the corpses' respective positions in the mass grave. The excavations were being done according to the book, to the letter of forensic science, so the survey had been done using twelve so-called "anatomical landmarks": the skull, wrists, elbows, shoulders, and other body parts. These plot the body position in three dimensions. This information was then fed into a computerized archaeological drawing package, in which the 3D image can be rotated through 360 degrees. By mapping the grave structure and the physical strata of the corpses, Hanson and Wright discerned how the bodies were physically placed in the graves along Čančari Road. The presence of a ramp, with attendant tire marks, demonstrated that the bodies were dumped in groups from tipper trucks and bulldozed in with a front loader. The tread and tool marks from these machines were measured and specified in size and shape so they could be matched to the perpetrators' machines like fingerprints if the vehicles themselves could be found.

Much of the different earth and surface material found scattered around the different graves was moved there by heavy earth-moving equipment, trucks, Caterpillar diggers, and bulldozers that had been used by the men who had buried the bodies back in summer 1995.

Fortunately, three years later, a few of these vehicles were still stand-ing in the same vehicle parks of the same, now mainly disused, mili-tary barracks scattered in the towns around Srebrenica, like Zvornik and Bijelina. And since the equipment was almost certainly unused since the operations between July and October 1995, then the bucket marks and tires of the machines could be matched to the tool marks and tracks in the graves. Wright realized the earth moved with the bodies to second-ary graves could also be cross-matched to the earth found in, on, and around the various primary burial sites such as the Petkovici Dam and Branjevo Farm. Tony Brown, a British environmental scientist, under-took matching soil profiles to provide evidence that the sites were linked. He came up with the pollen analysis of the soil that had been transferred from a field of wheat where executions had taken place. Traces of a rare volcanic rock found in one secondary grave led analysts using local geo-logical maps to realize that the rock could only have come from an out-crop situated above a single execution site. It was through such precise use of archaeological science and forensic principles that the team was able to link some of the different grave sites.

The Search for the Perpetrators

The work of those looking for the dead, meanwhile, was still moving much faster than the search for the living perpetrators. There was still no international agreement among countries like America, Britain, and France on how any arrest operations of war criminals should pro-ceed. Radovan Karadžić was still appearing publicly on television in the Republika Srpska. Mladić was still in Han Pijesak occasionally, but increasingly in Serbia. Human Rights Watch in New York estimated that by the time Hanson had arrived in Bosnia in 1997 only ten of the indicted Yugoslav war criminals had been arrested and transferred to The Hague. A French military intelligence officer was suspected of leak-ing to the Bosnian Serbs the details of an American-planned operation to arrest Radovan Karadžić in 1997 and 1998. But the worm was about to turn. At the NATO summit in Madrid at the beginning of July 1997, just two years after the beginning of the operation to take over Srebrenica, the Americans and the British found common cause. Gone was the Conservative regime of Prime Minister John Major. Great Britain had seen the election of Tony Blair in May that year, who had a more muscular approach to what became known as "an ethical foreign policy." Blair and Bill Clinton found common ground on the question of Bosnian and Serbian war criminals, and with Blair taking the lead with his new foreign secretary, Robin Cook, and encouraging the Americans, it was time to take action.

The proof of what the investigative teams were uncovering could not be ignored, and by now the international community both in Bosnia and elsewhere seemed to have noticeably changed their hands-off approach of 1996 and 1997. It had become obvious to the foreign administration of the Office of the High Representative, the senior NATO officers, and the diplomatic representatives of foreign governments in Bosnia that there was no way that the country could move forward politically, economically, or socially if the most notable war criminals were still at large. One example, among many, of this thinking had come from Britain's ambassador to Belgrade, Charles Crawford, a diplomat independent of spirit and inventive of mind, who had argued ceaselessly on this front since he had been the United Kingdom's diplomatic representative in Sarajevo between 1996 and 1998. In late 1996 he had sent a confidential telegram to London, in which he argued that what he called the "massively expensive British and Western investment in Bosnia" was "doomed to failure if action was not taken against the ICTY indictees, particularly the most senior ones."

He remembers his words and arguments being simple: "It made no sense for the international presence in Bosnia to go round trying to plant the green seeds of European reasonableness if a few paces behind us followed ICTY indictees pouring plant-killer on those seeds. London by then was coming to the same conclusion. A new policy was worked out with Washington, Clinton by then safely reelected, albeit at the risk of 'mission creep.' Specialist NATO troops would now take action to arrest and transfer to the ICTY all indictees."[9]

Crawford's argument, and the arguments of others, would bear fruit, having reached the right ears. NATO Special Forces teams would arrest a selection of those wanted by the ICTY, some of whom had been the subjects of "closed" or secret indictments. Among the first wanted men to be arrested would be those from in and around the town of Prijedor in northwestern Bosnia. Many of the Bosnian Muslim and Bosnian Croat inhabitants of the town and its surroundings had, in 1992, been detained in camps by the Bosnian Serbs of the newly formed Crisis Staff of the Municipality of Prijedor. The latter had seized control of Prijedor on April 30, 1992, making it part of the newly formed Serb Republic of Bosnia and Herzegovina. In May 1992, under artillery and tank shelling, infantry assaults of Bosnian Serb and JNA forces attacked Bosnian Muslim and Bosnian Croat areas in and around Prijedor: the civilians who survived this assault were rounded up and forced to march to three detention camps in the municipality. Omarska had been set up in an iron ore–mining complex east of Prijedor; Keraterm in the disused part of a ceramics factory; and Trnopolje, a series of buildings, including a school, cinema, and cultural center, in the village of the same name. Conditions in all three places were not good. An ICTY indictment of two of the men who ran the camp said:

> At Omarska prisoners were crowded together with little or no facilities for personal hygiene. They were fed starvation rations once a day and given only a few minutes to go to the canteen area, eat and then leave. The little water they received was often foul. Prisoners had no changes of clothing and no bedding. They received no medical care.

Killings and severe beatings of prisoners were commonplace. The camp guards, who were both police and military personnel, and others who came to the camp and physically abused the prisoners, used all manner of weapons during these beatings, including wooden batons, metal rods and tools, lengths of thick industrial cable, rifle butts and knives. Both female and male prisoners were beaten, raped, sexually assaulted, tortured and humiliated. Hundreds of the detainees, whose identities are known and unknown, did not survive the camp.[10]

One of the ICTY indictments was against two senior members of the Prijedor Crisis Committee, Simo Drljača and Milan Kovačević, charging them with complicity in the commission of genocide. The accused, read the indictment

> in concert with others, planned, instigated, and ordered the establishment of the camps at Omarska, Keraterm and Trnopolje and the detention therein of Bosnian Muslims and Bosnian Croats from the municipality of Prijedor under conditions calculated to bring about the physical destruction of the detainees, with the intent to destroy part of the Bosnian Muslim and Bosnian Croat groups, as such.

On the morning of July 10, 1997, Simo Drljača was fishing with his son and brother-in-law on the edges of Lake Gradine, a tree-fringed stretch of water halfway between Prijedor and the town of Omarska. What Drljača did not know was that he had been under observation from a ditch on one of the sides of the lake for several days by members of one of Britain's Special Forces units. When he heard the noise of incoming vehicles behind him, he made a move for a concealed handgun and turned, only to see British soldiers from the Special Air Service (SAS) coming toward him. He opened fire, hitting one of the SAS troopers; he was immediately shot four times, the bullets penetrating his heart, lungs, and liver. He was dead on the spot.

Almost simultaneously, in a continuation of the operation code-named "Tango," another team from the SAS negotiated their way into Prijedor hospital and seized its director, Milan Kovačević, included in the indictment with Drljača. He came quietly and was transferred to the US Eagle Airbase outside Tuzla, and thence onward to The Hague.

Other arrest operations took place, but then came the coup de grace. On December 2, 1998, General Radislav Krstić, one of Mladić's key deputies, was traveling inside the Republika Srpska in northern Bosnia. Despite being an internationally indicted war criminal, he felt free to move around at will—until balaclava-clad soldiers from the 22 SAS Regiment with backup from a Navy SEAL unit blocked off his convoy and disabled his Audi with spikes on a road in the village of Vrsari, as he was en route to Banja Luka on business. The British soldiers smashed the windows of his car with sledgehammers before pulling him through the broken glass, and the general's humiliation was completed when his false leg, the result of a landmine injury, reportedly came off.

And Ratko Mladić? By now he had largely left his barracks outside Han Pijesak and moved across the Drina River into Serbia, where he was to receive, for now, the hospitality of the Serbian military and authorities.

Chapter Five

INSIDE KOSOVO, SERBIA, AND THE WORLD OF THE MISSING

By 1999, a year had passed since Ian Hanson, Richard Wright, and the rest of the ICTY exhumation team had stood at the Petkovici Dam and realized that the network of secondary grave sites from the Srebrenica massacre was far more extensive than they had expected. The newly born International Commission on Missing Persons also realized that the number of missing from the wars in the former Yugoslavia was much larger than they had thought. The list included people of every ethnicity. The suffering of Bosnia was universal, not divided by ethnic lines. There were Serbs from the Krajina in the west of Bosnia who had gone missing during the Croat military offensive in 1995; there were Croats who had gone missing in 1991 at the hands of the Serbs in Vukovar and eastern Slavonia; and there were Bosnian Muslims who had disappeared in and around Prijedor in northwestern Bosnia in 1993. And that was just the start. There were missing persons, civilians and combatants, from all parts of Bosnia, victims of all three ethnicities who had disappeared in the fighting that had swept over the region since 1991.

The map of the former Yugoslavia was a map of the missing, and everyone was affected. It was estimated that roughly 83 percent of the missing were Bosnian Muslims, nearly 12 percent Serb, and about 5 percent Croat.[1] These numbers were, of course, open to massive inter-pretation, argument, dispute, muted acceptance, and ferocious denial by the missing persons organizations associated with each ethnic group-ing. These organizations were, at the start, fractured along ethnic and regional lines. There were two different missing persons commissions as well—one in the Federation, another in the Republika Srpska—and at the beginning each of them only had the authority to look for miss-ing persons on their own territory. Many of the Bosnian Muslim people who had gone missing in the Republika Srpska—around Srebrenica, for example—were buried there. And many Serbs who had gone missing were buried in areas where their missing persons commission could not go looking for them.

The search was on to find a state-level organization that could han-dle not just the search for the missing persons, but other social and legal aspects of the issue, regardless of the territorial division of the entities or ethnic origin of the relatives of victims. But this was contentious territory. It was only a few years after the war, and in this politically and psychoso-cially charged arena, the more ethnic egalitarianism was introduced, the more entropic was the effect on all three sides. This atmosphere also fre-quently affected the work of the national and international professionals who had come offering forensic and human rights assistance.

This field of scientific and human rights specialization had formed out of the South and Central American dictatorships and guerilla wars of the 1970s and 1980s, when thousands of people had been forcibly disappeared at the hands of government troops, police, or death squads. This problem was by no means limited to South America. The conflict in Cyprus in the 1960s and 1970s had resulted in more than 2,000 missing persons. Several thousand more went missing in Kosovo between 1997 and 1999. The genocide in Rwanda in 1994 and the subsequent conflicts in Burundi and the Democratic Republic of the Congo between 1993 and 1997 had left thousands upon thousands of people missing. There was also Lebanon, Vietnam, and South Africa from the apartheid days, as well as the missing of the Iran–Iraq war and the First Gulf War.

Another important influence was Chechnya, with its missing civilians killed by the Russians and the Russian soldiers taken prisoner by the Chechen rebels. And then there was the conflict-churned red earth of the Great Lakes region of central Africa, which included Rwanda, Burundi, and the former Zaire. The figures there were sometimes rounded up to the nearest large round number. The latter, now named the Democratic Republic of the Congo (DRC), saw a new conflict starting in 1998, to be dubbed "Africa's First World War." When the time came to add up the dead, one leading humanitarian agency, the International Rescue Committee, put a huge amount of work into the business of assessing the death toll. It was to report that between 1998 and 2007 the number of deaths from battle, atrocities, disease, and malnutrition in the DRC could exceed 5 million.[2]

What made each of these instances different, besides the numbers and the geographical locations, was the way in which the governments in the countries in question tried to solve or avoid the issue.

Dealing with the issue of missing persons can be problematic and tricky, especially when the governments or regimes in power in a particular country can be linked to the crimes. The authorities of the Republika Srpska in Bosnia in 1999 had a very large number of missing Bosnian Muslim persons buried on their territory, there were Serbs whose remains were found on—or more precisely under—the ground in the Muslim-Croat Federation, and Kosovo Albanians ended up buried inside Serbia while Kosovo Serbs were interred in areas controlled by Kosovo Albanians.

So before organizations like the ICMP could deploy an approach based upon forensic science, human rights, and rule of law, the different governments in question would have to take responsibility for the problem, decide on accountability, and ask for help. Regardless of whether it was the ICMP, the International Committee of the Red Cross, or other agencies who were involved in providing assistance, the governments had to ask for help first.

Enter the ICMP

The International Commission on Missing Persons had humble beginnings. By 1999 it had been up and running for just over a year, primarily as a small political organization advocating that the issue of missing persons in Bosnia and Herzegovina had to be dealt with, and that governments, such as the new one in Bosnia, needed assistance in tackling it. There was, at the start, a handful of international and hastily recruited Bosnian staff, metaphorically standing in front of the muddy, decomposing, disarticulated results of every massacre and large-scale killing of the whole Bosnian war, wondering where to start. Meanwhile, right in front of them, in the villages, towns, cities, fields, and valleys of Bosnia were thousands of women like Kada Hotic looking to them for answers.

The ICMP's small office was in the center of Sarajevo, which after four years of artillery, mortar, and cannon fire looked as though a huge pack of giant, angry bears had swiped their paws across every piece of architecture and masonry in the city. Some buildings were burned-out shells, while some were riddled with machine-gun fire but fully intact, a tribute to their solid, Austro-Hungarian design and construction. One of the ICMP's senior expatriate staff was Kathryne Bomberger, a tenacious American who had previously worked in government and media circles in Washington, DC. She had crossed over into the human rights arena, and after a stint in Haiti in 1994 she found herself working for a large international organization in Bosnia. Immediately after the Bosnian war, she was based in Foca, a small town on the Drina River, downriver from Srebrenica and upriver from Goražde. She had been thrown in at the proverbial deep end. The town had been the wartime headquarters for some of the worst Serbian paramilitaries.

Before the war, Foca had been a pleasant, riverside town, but during the war, it became synonymous with one word: rape. Bosnian women kidnapped and taken prisoner by Bosnian Serb paramilitary groups—for example, the White Eagles of Vojislav Šešelj—were kept as sex slaves and prostitutes in sports halls, motels, and private houses, existing to service Bosnian Serbs on their way to, and back from, the front. One Bosnian woman taken prisoner outside Mostar by the White Eagles described afterward how she was first gang-raped multiple times and then sent to work in a brothel in Foca where she was forced to assume a Serbian name to please the drunken ethnic cleansers who made up her clients.

The 1995 Dayton Accords included clauses for dealing with missing persons: initially, it was to be handled by the Geneva-based International Committee of the Red Cross. Dayton said that all parties signatory to it should cooperate with the ICRC in finding missing persons. Then, after the G7 summit in Lyons, which saw the founding of the organization, the ICMP was mandated to become involved with dealing with the enormous issue too. And so at the beginning, a deputy chief of staff from the ICRC was appointed to serve with the ICMP for a time. The two organizations, one with a humanitarian approach and the other based on the rule of law, both worked on the problem for a time, in their different ways, sometimes separately and sometimes cooperatively. The ICRC, based in Switzerland, was, in essence, a kind of practical guardian of the Geneva Conventions—this was the world's de facto international humanitarian law, what can be called the laws of war.

The ICRC was bound to make sure the conventions were upheld and respected worldwide, in places from Chechnya to Mali, from Kosovo to Gaza. Their operational activities included things like visiting prisons, distributing aid, evacuating victims of atrocities and those in humanitarian need, arranging cease-fires, and bearing witness to the world's darkest moments. They tended to the wounded, educated soldiers and commanders in the legal aspects of the rules of war, and when the Geneva Conventions were being violated, sounded the alarm. They had stayed behind, along with Doctors Without Borders, in the blood-splattered machete madness of the Rwandan genocide, after everyone else had pulled out. Very often they were the first humanitarians into countries at war—and the last ones out.

The ICRC might have been long on conventions, treaties, rules, and legislation—they were, after all, Swiss—but they were not short on bravery, speaking out, toeing the legal line, or putting their operational money where their organizational mouth was. So in Bosnia and Croatia, as well as in Kosovo, in 1999 the ICRC dealt with the various humanitarian aspects of the thousands of missing persons cases. The ICMP, with its emphasis on the rule of law and with DNA identification as the first step toward that end, brought along a new approach and a new solution to the problem. And there was an important factor that could not be overlooked during the multiple changes that occurred as the ICMP started helping governments worldwide deal with the issue of missing persons: this issue had to fall not just under the umbrella of humanitarianism, but also increasingly under one of human rights and the rule of law.

By this time, thousands of victims were being exhumed from mass graves in Bosnia, where from 1996 to 1999 6,353 "cases"—body bags containing a collection of individually separate human remains making up parts of one body, be it one bone or two hundred—had been recovered. The evidence of "fact of death" that the investigators from The Hague had been looking for had not been in short supply around Srebrenica. This evidence came from the secondary grave sites, the primary execution sites, and the primary burial sites. Of all of these, there were some 50 main ones,[3] of which the primary sites and execution sites were found first. The multiple secondary sites followed, with some being discovered reasonably quickly and others taking years to uncover. Other smaller mass graves were found too. The bigger sites yielded layer after layer of machine-gunned cadavers in various states of decomposition, bullets in their decaying bodies, almost all in civilian clothes, and many of them with their arms bound behind their backs with ligatures made from cloth, wire, or dark grey-green military telephone wire as issued to the Yugoslav National Army. After being exhumed, the bodies were placed in body bags and then taken to the appropriate mortuary facility. Finding a proper place to store the remains was not always easy—at one point the bags were stored in containers set up close to the exhumation sites. The issue of forensic practicality had to be balanced out with due thought and respect for the families whose relatives were contained in the black and white plastic and polythene bags. With a proper system not yet in place, problems and protests were bound to arise—at one point bodies had to be stored in the Clinical Centre in Tuzla, where the staff, not surprisingly, horrified by the appalling smell, threatened to go on strike. In due course, somewhere else was found as a storage area for the thousands of body parts being exhumed from the Srebrenica mass graves: the salt mines in Tuzla.

The city of Tuzla had a long history of political and social independence. During the war, following the example of its egalitarian and fair-minded mayor, it had tried to remain as neutral as possible, thus avoiding much of the violence that swept the rest of the country.

Tuzla was (and still is) a manufacturing town, with its chief industry, opencast coal mining for a huge power plant, dominating the economic landscape. However, the town's other industrial mainstay was salt mining, and there were tunnels bored into the rocky slopes surrounding the municipality. It was in these tunnels that the bodies were first stored, partly because there was nowhere else to put them, and because they were at least lying somewhere with a consistent temperature. However, in short order, rats moved into these makeshift tunnel morgues. When Kathryne Bomberger, by then the co–chief of staff of the ICMP, heard about the invasion of rodents, she decided enough was enough, and so, under her auspices, the world's first "super mortuary," a building large enough to hold the different remains of hundreds of bodies, was built in the parking lot of a funeral home in Tuzla.

Finding the Family of Kada Hotic

When she came to the ICMP, Kada Hotic wasn't quite sure what the organization's purpose was. She attended meetings held by it and the ICRC, among other groups. And, like many things in Bosnia just after the war, she'd heard of the organization through word of mouth from the closely interlinked network of widows and surviving relatives of the menfolk of Srebrenica. These relatives had by now formed themselves into a large and strident organization, based in Sarajevo and Tuzla, called the Mothers of the Enclaves of Srebrenica and Žepa. Like similar associations across the Balkans, the group fought for families' rights, pushed for identifications of the missing, and tried to establish a proper, permanent place of burial for the victims' remains. Across the former Yugoslavia, but particularly in Bosnia, relatives demanding to know the location of their menfolk were forming dozens of these associations. They'd taken the example of the mothers of the *desaparecidos*, the "disappeared," in Central and South America, where such advocate groups were an acknowledged social force.

Kada was looking for her two brothers, Ekrem and Mustafa, her husband Sejad, and her son Samir. She had a daughter, Lejla, who was now married with a child and lived just outside Sarajevo working as a pharmacist. Kada, like many Bosnians, was initially skeptical when she heard about the ICMP and how it claimed to be able to help. She and her friends and colleagues knew that the ICRC had been able to give some form of limited help by matching clothing and personal items taken from bodies, and by collecting photographs of such items in large picture books for the families to look at. But these foreigners from the ICMP? According to many Bosnian women with missing relatives, the organization's techniques sounded newfangled and suspicious. Like many of her fellow countrymen, Kada Hotic had a low view of much of the international community by the end of the 1990s. She looked at them in the same way she viewed interlopers such as the UN, NATO, and the European Union, all of whom had promised to protect Bosnian civilians during the war. As far as Kada saw it, the only people who had helped her during the war had been the Red Cross, Doctors Without Borders, and eventually, the Americans. The latter had taken the aerial photos of Srebrenica; many Bosnians had heard about how Madeleine Albright had waved the photos at the UN, trying to bring attention to the massacre. It had been the Americans who had pushed to end the war with airstrikes as well.

Some Bosnians understood why the international community had acted as it had. Others tended to take a more cynical view, recalling their experiences of Dutch UN soldiers drinking *slivovitz* and fraternizing with the Serbs when they entered Srebrenica, or the international bureaucrats who, by not dealing with Ratko Mladić's forces militarily, had allowed the siege of Sarajevo to continue as long as it had.

There were thousands of people like Kada across Bosnia: Muslim, Croat, and Serbian women who'd lost their husbands, sons, fathers, uncles, and cousins. And in the years that followed the war, they were reporting their missing relatives to the ICMP, to the ICRC, and to the two commissions that dealt with missing persons in the Federation and in the Republika Srpska. Eventually, the figure of persons missing in Bosnia alone was to stand somewhere between 28,000 and 30,000.

The killers, meanwhile, were on the receiving end of the judicial processes of The Hague Tribunal. By 1999 the court had extended its mandate to include crimes committed in Kosovo. Ratko Mladić, Radovan Karadžić, and others were now sharing the dubious honor of having been indicted for genocide with then–Serbian president Slobodan Milošević, indicted for the actions taken by his forces against Albanians in Kosovo. Milošević was to be subsequently indicted for crimes committed in Croatia and Bosnia.

Inside Kosovo and Serbia

It was summer 1999, and another Balkan conflict, this time in Kosovo, was, like glacial ice, cracking with a dry, sharp report, tearing the region apart. In the southern Serbian province 200 miles southeast of Bosnia, Milošević's soldiers and paramilitaries had been tearing up the human rights rulebook since 1998 while clamping down against secession-minded Kosovo Albanians, who made up the province's majority. The latter had formed their own guerilla army, the Kosovo Liberation Army, which had clashed repeatedly with Serbian forces across the oak forests and scrubby hills of the tiny province. The Serbs replied with excessive force against the Albanian civilian population, as in the small western Kosovar village of Bela Crkva. In the days after the NATO bombing campaign on Serbia that started on the night of March 24, 1999, some 60 Kosovo Albanian civilians were executed there. Serb forces carried out the killings near a small river that flows through fields of peppers, onions, and maize south of the village. One local Albanian farmer, who lost several members of his family in the killing, helped bury the bodies immediately afterward. He also made his own impromptu memorial to the dead, particularly the small children machine-gunned in the massacre. Inside a thicket of hazel branches in one of the fields by the river, he hung two tiny pairs of colored Wellington boots that he'd removed from two of the corpses of the children who'd been shot.[4]

Richard Holbrooke and other American negotiators traveled between Belgrade and Pristina, the Kosovar regional capital, trying to negotiate a halt to the violence. Milošević, in the style of Bosnian Serb leaders, broke promises and made false assurances, while his men continued to kill Kosovo Albanian civilians and forced others to flee into neighboring Macedonia, Albania, and Montenegro. With the lessons of Bosnia very clear in their minds, NATO leaders lost patience very quickly, and by March 1999 the skies over southeastern Europe were crisscrossed with vapor trails of NATO jets bombing targets in Serbia and its southern breakaway province of Kosovo. Milošević gave in after 78 days while Serb troops, and some 100,000 Serb civilians, pulled northward out of Kosovo, back to Serbia proper. Forty-five thousand NATO troops poured into Kosovo to keep the peace and build the world's newest nation-state.

Milošević's forces left the evidence behind. At the Erturi coffee bar in the southern town of Suva Reka, the interior was a familiar scene of blood-spattered walls, torched furniture, and Kalashnikov cartridge cases.

Serbian police officers had forced a group of some twenty-plus Albanian women, children, and elderly men inside the bar, thrown in hand grenades, and machine-gunned the interior. The victims' bodies were loaded onto a dump truck, from which a survivor managed to jump and hide. The corpses were buried in the local garbage dump by Roma gypsies paid for the night's work, then dug up and buried on a military firing range, then exhumed a second time and driven back to Serbia in one of a number of freezer lorries. With a hefty rock jammed against the accelerator, the lorry was driven into the River Danube. The killers were trying to hide the evidence again.[5] The missing Kosovo Serbs and Kosovo Albanians from the conflict were added to the list of missing persons from the Balkan wars of the 1990s.

After the wars in Croatia and Bosnia and the conflict in Kosovo, Serbia found itself being treated as a pariah, largely because of the excesses carried out by the Milošević regime in neighboring countries and in Kosovo. It was the normal people of Serbia who paid for it. They were enduring internationally imposed sanctions against the Belgrade government. Travel in and out of the country was difficult without the requisite visas. Foreign currency for the average population was in short supply, even as Milošević stripped the state coffers, flying huge amounts of cash abroad to banks in countries like Cyprus. NATO, the international community, and everybody else were keenly aware of how easily conflict could break out again. Around Kosovo's boundaries—it was still a part of Serbia, so the demarcation lines were referred to as "boundaries" instead of "borders"—was a five-kilometer-wide stretch of land, sealed on both sides with barbed wire and guarded by armed troops. In one American army outpost overlooking a stretch of this boundary zone, tanks pointed their barrels toward the green fields and oak clumps of Serbia's Presevo Valley. This barrier zone was called the "exclusion zone," and neither NATO nor Serb troops were allowed into it, in order to reduce the possibilities of confrontation. At a time when Serbia's nationalist authorities had their backs against the wall, it was easy to understand why a nationalist hero like Ratko Mladić, who'd reportedly driven across the Drina River one foggy afternoon just after the arrest of Radislav Krstić, was finding it so easy to live freely in the Serbian capital and in barracks and facilities owned by the country's military.

Milošević had, on Mladić's arrival in Belgrade, welcomed him and decided to protect him from the ICTY. Milošević himself had been indicted, and he saw Mladić as a national hero of the Bosnian wars who needed the assistance of the Serbian state. Milošević also wanted to know where Mladić was at any given time since Mladić knew everything about links between the Belgrade administration of the Serbian government and the Bosnian Serb government and army during the war. The intelligence services of the former Yugoslavia had sprung out of the operational ethos of Marshal Tito's units during World War II and had been honed during the Cold War when Yugoslavia was spying on (and being spied on by) all of its neighbors. So Milošević made it the job of a number of former and serving soldiers and intelligence agents to look after Mladić.

The Serbs felt historically misunderstood and victimized. The majority of citizens who had little or no control over their lives saw themselves being drawn into wars by their political leaders. During Tito's reign, the Yugoslav intelligence services had also faced off against the Russians, the Hungarians, the Albanians, and the West. During the Bosnian war, they opposed NATO, which mainly meant the Americans. And in the aftermath of the Kosovo bombings, they were once again up against the domestic, military, and foreign intelligence assets of the 41 different countries that had contributed soldiers and police officers to NATO's Kosovo Force (KFOR) and the United Nations Mission in Kosovo (UNMIK), the province's de facto international overseers. Serbia saw itself, understandably, under a triangulation of threats to its territory and people: from the investigators of the ICTY, from NATO forces determined to keep Kosovo and Bosnia in some form of stable peace, and from the secessionist Republic of Montenegro. It also particularly stung that Serbia had lost its spiritual heartland of Kosovo, the cradle of the Serbian Orthodox Church, with its monasteries and churches, to NATO and the Albanians.

It is easy to understand how law-abiding civilians felt victimized, living in a country that was bombed every night for over three months by the most powerful military alliance in the world. And the Serbs had a point: their country seemed to be getting smaller. They'd lost Kosovo, they were losing Montenegro, and government buildings in Belgrade and other cities were still being blasted to ruins by NATO's aerial bombs. A popular joke at the time went: "What do Nokia and Serbia have in common?" Answer: "Each year there's a smaller model."

But according to the Serbs, Kosovo was historically part of Serbia, and would always be. The Serbian approach to land they see as rightfully belonging to them is summed up, not entirely untruthfully, by this typically black-humored and popular Balkans joke told by everybody from Serbs to Croats to Bosnians to Albanians, always with the Serb as the nationalist fall guy:

> To qualify for entry to the European Union, Albania, Serbia, Croatia, and Bosnia have to come up with a workable, multi-ethnic space program,

democratically focused and in keeping with all of the endless standards of sustainability, gender mainstreaming, and diversity quotas that Brussels bureaucrats always seem to insist on. So a spaceship is built and the mission launched. And one Sunday, the four men land on Mars. The Albanian is first out of the door. He takes one look at the landscape, the hills and rocks, and immediately proclaims that it looks like central Albania, and therefore Mars must thenceforth belong to his country. The Bosnian looks at the rocky features of the red planet, comments immediately that it looks like rocky Herzegovina, and therefore must be Bosnian. The Croat sniffs, sees there is no Catholic church in sight, and gets back in the spaceship. Meanwhile, the Serb looks around, stretches, and pulls a knife out of his pocket. Stabbing himself in the chest, he watches his blood dribble down onto the rocks.

"Ha!" he cries. "It's simple. *Srpska zemlja*! Wherever Serbian blood is shed, then that is Serbian land!"

People laughed, but it was true.

However, there was little humor about the operation to look after and protect Ratko Mladić. The general, still a serving soldier in 2000, was renting a four-floor house in the residential Belgrade suburb of Košutnjak, at number 117a on Blagoja Parovica Street.[6] It was near the Topcider military barracks where Mladić went to volunteer his assistance during operations in and around Kosovo. It was close, too, to the military hospital, whose director, Zoran Stankovic, had performed the autopsy on Mladić's 23-year-old daughter Ana when she shot herself in the head with one of the general's pistols in 1994. As his daughter lay on her deathbed, Mladić asked to be allowed to keep both a lock of her hair and the pistol bullet extracted from her skull.[7]

Mladić was seen watching a football match; walking around town; having dinner in a popular restaurant; praying at his daughter's grave; meeting with army colleagues and friends like Zdravko Tolimir, also indicted by the ICTY; and openly welcoming family friends to his son's wedding and his grandchildren's christening.

Despite their very loud and verbal protests, their denouncements of NATO, and the apparent deification of Mladić by their more hardcore elements, the Serbs, and the Bosnian Serbs in particular, knew very well that at least a sizeable proportion of the dead and missing in Bosnia were Bosnian Muslims, however much they might have wanted to challenge the numbers or dispute the events surrounding their deaths. Many Bosnian Serbs, isolated or displaced during the war, might not have even known about the killings at Srebrenica before 2004. Apart from anything else, this was a period when Internet access in much of Serbia was in its infancy. Most only knew what was in the newspaper, on television, or on the radio, or what they gleaned from conversation and gossip. So they would not necessarily have been aware that the majority of the 11,000-odd casualties in Kosovo were not just civilians, but also Kosovo Albanians.

But outside players, apart from the media, had been documenting what had been happening to the Serbs in their country. The reports from Human Rights Watch on the Kosovo conflict were characteristically accurate and methodical, recording not just crimes committed by both sides against each other, but also civilian casualties of NATO's bombing campaign: there were some 90 incidents of Serbian and Albanian civilians killed or wounded by missiles or bombs launched from the sky. Civilians died when a train from Belgrade to Thessaloniki in Greece was mistakenly hit by an air-launched missile as it crossed a bridge that NATO was targeting. In another instance, a retirement home was hit. NATO even mistakenly deployed ordnance in the vicinity of a convoy inside Kosovo carrying Albanian refugees, the very people they were operating to save.

So it may have come easier for many Bosnian Serb and Serb civilians to adopt the psychosocial mantle of the victim, instead of the perpetrator—the role they felt was the preserve of their government and army. Serbs believed that the international community was always going to treat them as the enemies, the wrongdoers, mostly on behalf of what their leaders had done. Several things had confirmed this to them at that point. The operational and financial sympathy that the international community was extending towards the Muslim-Croat Federation in Bosnia far exceeded, they felt, what the Serbs were receiving; NATO had bombed them in Serbia; and the information surrounding the increasing number of bodies emerging from exhumations around Srebrenica pointed directly toward Serb involvement. The innocent majority of Serbs could see that they were going to be blamed for the actions of a very small number of hardliners who had carried out this massacre and others.

American, British, Dutch, German, French, and Norwegian bombers and fighter jets had spent 78 days in the spring of 1999 flying from aircraft carriers in the Adriatic and NATO airbases on the eastern Italian seaboard. They'd dropped their payloads onto President Milošević's paramilitaries and soldiers rampaging across Kosovo, as well as onto government buildings, radio communications sites, and military infrastructures in the rest of Serbia. The aim was to halt the killing inside Kosovo, to allow hundreds of thousands of Kosovo Albanian refugees to return home, and to bomb Milošević to the negotiating table. The Serbs accused NATO of hitting civilians and of deliberately targeting the Chinese embassy in Belgrade, killing Chinese diplomats and Serb civilians.[8]

All sides in the conflict used propaganda as a weapon. One of the most original examples was in Kosovo in the summer of 1999, just after NATO had entered the province, when the Serbs were either stuck in enclaves or fleeing en masse to north of the River Ibar, close to the boundary with Serbia. Counterfeit pink Bazooka bubble gum was frequently given in Kosovo Albanian stores by shopkeepers as a substitute for small change, deutschmark coins being in short supply. The moment their province was liberated, Kosova Albanians had immediately rejected the hated Yugoslav dinar, replacing it with the German deutschmark. Sandwiched in between the outer wrapper and the gum itself would be small photographs of atrocities committed against Albanians. They also showed pictures of Kosovo Liberation Army guerilla fighters and NATO tanks and airplanes. One photo in one piece of "atrocity gum" showed an old Albanian man lying on a sheepskin on a sofa, shot in the head, his brains splattered on the wall behind him. Even when buying sweets, political points were being made, those unwrapping the gum being reminded of what had happened in Kosovo.

The events in Bosnia, Kosovo, Serbia, and elsewhere were, naturally, going to be the subject of acceptance, denial, and distortion in the media and in popular thinking. Revisionist history and denial of atrocities sprung up on all sides, not just in and after the Balkan wars, but as it does after almost all conflicts. Many people deal with unpalatable truths, and events for which they have no explanation, through conspiracy theories. It is a favored narrative tool that is often used when it comes to genocide and mass death. Numbers are considered falsified or exaggerated. Witnesses and protagonists, and participants or victims, have their narration of events dismissed by any side that disagrees with them, which normally means the opposite side. Conspiracy theories the world over are similar because they tend to blame events on a greater, hidden plan rather than on a more easily explained prosaic reality. They are also prevalent in regions like the Balkans because they allow the individual to have their own fixed opinions about the historical narrative, about how many people died, which side suffered the most (almost always the individual's in question), and what the terrible dark conspiracy behind events actually was. In the former Yugoslavia, where intellectual and political dissent had been quashed under Tito, and then in the nineties the war came, many people had too little control over their lives.

So having your own conspiratorial opinions—however barmy the facts that backed them up—lent people an air of individuality.

The conspiracy theory is also a familiar concept in the Balkans because so often the information vacuum, left dry and bereft on a diet of politically biased and party-*pris* media, is filled with distorted rumor, revisionist history, and information invented to fill the gap. "My truth is always greater than your truth" is a common regional mindset. And there was no greater challenge to a conspiratorial mindset than allegations that one side committed a genocide against another, hid the evidence, and tried to get away with it. And so the increasing numbers of dead from Srebrenica who were to be exhumed, and then identified, played very strongly into the conspiratorial nature of those who would deny and detract from the reality of what actually happened there. It made no difference that the cutting edge of modern science was being used to identify the victims not just of Srebrenica, but also of every conflict across the Balkans, utterly regardless of ethnic calling. This was one of the subsidiary battles that the ICMP had to fight, not just in the Balkans, but everywhere the problem of missing persons persisted. When President Clinton said that the ICMP would be tasked with providing an accurate accounting of the missing, part of the task included extinguishing the damaging flames of distorted history.

The conspiratorial mindset described above is an example of binary thinking—a phrase often deployed in comparative discussions about genocide—that says every event or argument has to be reduced to two ways of thinking: good and bad, black and white, heroic or evil. It is an argumentative technique that does not allow for the existence of two varying degrees of right or wrong, or varying degrees of anything. It certainly does not allow for the existence of a middle ground of reason or compromise, the latter being seen to be akin to raising the white flag of surrender. If my truth is greater than your truth, then what on earth could there possibly be to compromise about?

A perfect example of binary thinking also says that there can only really be one true victim of any event. This narrative suggests an attack on the whole is an attack on the individual, and in binary thinking everything devolves back to the individual. This leads to another mind-set sometimes common among less objective people in post-conflict areas. This is the ability to take offense at an unpalatable truth. One saying goes: "Any slight, however slight, will be taken as a slight, and if there is no slight, then that in itself is a slight."

This way of thinking in turn leads to the removal of any possible objectivity in any argument—which pushes arguments to polar extremes, creating further confrontation. A Burundian army colonel in 1995 warned this author about the perils of investigating too closely killings of civilians allegedly carried out by the Burundian military. When challenged and told that the careful reporting of possible atrocities carried out by both sides contributed to a balanced, and moderate, approach to journalism, the colonel stated that "moderation is in itself a form of extremism."[9] Binary thinking again, an inability to recognize that wrongs done to and by each side are just that: wrong.

Given the approach to discourse described above, it would not be unfair to say that the regional narrative stage in the Balkans, in the aftermath of the wars of the 1990s, was hardly set for an open and frank exchange of views on such issues as recent history, identity, and genocide. So a part of the ICMP's work was to create, establish, and manage truth about what had happened to the thousands of missing persons, basing their accounts on established, sourced truth and the findings of modern science.

Meanwhile the NATO bombing campaign had hideous realities for the Serbian and Albanian civilians. Still, as a nation under attack from the air, the Serbs proved in a kind of impressive Balkans Blitz spirit that they had a sense of humor. Postcards quickly appeared in Belgrade during the NATO bombing campaign with an illustration of the American

Stealth bomber, supposedly invisible to radar, shot down by a Cold War–era piece of equipment. "Sorry, we didn't know it was invisible," read the caption. Graffiti appeared in the northwestern Serbian town of Novi Sad, where a NATO aircraft hit the bridge over the Danube. "It's OK," read the graffiti, "we never wanted to go to the other side anyway." Another example was a photograph postcard that reportedly appeared in 1999. It's taken of a typically good-looking Serbian woman in the warmth of early summer, wearing a white t-shirt with, very visibly, nothing underneath it. "Stealth Bra," reads the caption. Humor, victimhood, eternal disagreement over whose truth is more legitimate, whose land is whose, whose version of history is correct, and who's in the right: the issues have overlapped in the Balkans forever. *U zemlji krvi I meda*, as people said, which translates as "in the land of blood and honey."[10]

However, any black humor was not in evidence when ethnic Serbs from both sides of the Drina River gathered to discuss Holland's "kangaroo court," as it was often called, which they felt had been set up strictly to target them. While NATO troops might be able to arrest ICTY indictees inside Bosnia, Mladić and Milošević felt they were safe in Belgrade with their subordinates, friends, and the entire apparatus of Serbdom around them. Their supporters thought that Serbia had in recent history never been so unified against the outside world. Though there was a reward on Mladić's head of $5 million offered by the US State Department, he felt confident that no Serb would betray him, partly out of national pride, but also because of fear of repercussions.

Meanwhile, those who had hidden the bodies of the Srebrenica victims had done so to make sure that no proper evidence would ever surface. But across the Drina, unbeknownst to these men behind the reburial operations, new forms of identification for the remains of missing persons were about to start revolutionizing the whole arena of war crimes and human rights abuses.

In places like Bosnia, Argentina, Cyprus, and Guatemala, prior to 2001, identifications of missing persons whose decomposed and decomposing bodies had been exhumed from mass graves had been made by so-called "traditional" means. This involved relatives examining clothing taken off the recovered corpses, as well as looking at dental records and such personal artifacts as jewelry and identity papers. This had been the initial approach taken in Bosnia by both the ICMP and the International Committee of the Red Cross. So when the bodies from the Srebrenica killings, and others, were exhumed, the clothes were removed from the bodies, and all of the attendant personal possessions that the victims had been carrying with them or on them when they died were collected too. These included watches, rings, identity documents, combs, dentures, spectacles, tape cassettes, tobacco tins, lighters, notebooks, and money. Their clothing was muddy, bloodstained, and smeared with the effluent liquids that accompanied the decomposition of their corpses. There were shoes, anoraks, jumpers, jeans, socks, jackets, underwear, and shirts. The ICMP, the two different missing persons commissions from the Republika Srpska and the Muslim-Croat Federation, and the ICRC photographed the clothing and possessions. Huge books were compiled that relatives of missing persons queued to look at in the hope of identifying the bodies that had worn the clothes or carried the possessions. Exhibitions of photographs were shown in Sarajevo and the main towns of Bosnia, Croatia, Kosovo, and Serbia.

But by late 1999 and early 2000, the ICMP's forensic experts were very skeptical about using material remains and clothing for reliable identifications. This way of doing things—the AM and PM or ante-mortem and post-mortem, method—was deeply flawed, and cautious estimates had proven that it could lead to substantial misidentification rates. In Kosovo in 2002, this author witnessed two Kosovo Albanian families engaged in a screaming match over a pair of muddy jeans exhumed from a mass grave, both sides adamant that the trousers had belonged to one of their relatives. So, when several different Bosnian individuals identified the same pair of jeans taken from one secondary mass grave of Srebrenica victims on Čančari Road as belonging to their own missing relative, it was time to admit that the AM and PM method would not be effective. Of the non-Srebrenica-related cases exhumed in Bosnia, it had also proven possible to identify only 65 percent of the bodies. The rate of inaccurate identifications was probably very high; the ICMP suspected as high as 30 percent. With few reliable identifications being made, family associations of missing persons' relatives clamoring for results, and an enormous backlog of unidentified corpses, something had to be done. The ICMP knew that a completely new identification system had to be developed, one that could guarantee results. For this, the International Commission on Missing Persons was looking at three letters: DNA.

Chapter Six

BUILDING A HUMAN IDENTIFICATION SYSTEM

B efore he took the job as director of administration and finance at the International Commission on Missing Persons, Adam Boys had already had two near-death experiences in Bosnia. One was in a bad traffic accident, and the second was while working as an international monitor on the mountainous Bosnian border with Montenegro during the war as the leader of a team of foreign observers keeping an eye on any suspect movements of anything across the frontier. The highly personable and determined former chartered accountant from the west of Scotland had fallen foul of a Montenegrin police chief named Striko. The chief didn't like Boys and didn't like the fact that the stockily built and unassuming man from Glasgow wouldn't let him use the foreign monitors' official jeeps to ferry the Montenegrin policemen on lengthy drinking sessions to neighboring towns. Things came to a head when Boys confiscated the keys of his jeep from a catastrophically drunk Striko one evening, preventing the latter from taking his men for another round of beers and *rakiya*, the local brandy. The tiny statelet of Montenegro was at the time part of Serbia, as they had formed a union in 1992 out of the two remaining republics of Yugoslavia. The Montenegrin officer saw Boys and his team as just another hated adjunct of the international community. So in response to Boys, he drew his pistol, pointed it directly at the Scotsman's head, and pulled the trigger. There was a dull click. The drunken officer had no round in the weapon's chamber.[1]

Boys came from strong stock: his maternal grandfather had fled Denmark during World War II to join the British Royal Navy to fight against the Germans, and his father's family came from the rugged west of Scotland. Two crucial things were in Boys's professional blood that were to prove of enormous assistance to the nascent ICMP: first, a background in accounting, and second, a strong strain of dedication to public service inherited from the Danish side of the family and from his paternal grandfather, who was a church minister. Prior to his arrival at the International Commission on Missing Persons, Boys worked in Sarajevo at the Office of the High Representative, whose mandated task was the upkeep of the Dayton Peace Accords. He was taken on to make the financial management, administration, and operating procedures of the ICMP commensurate with a fully fledged and properly functioning international organization. When he arrived, the newly established outfit was small and primarily political. The key staff had, he said, "superb commitment and an excellent idea, and the goal was to convert the vision into reality." But what the ICMP really needed was money, meaning international donations and support. It was not easy to persuade international governmental donors to part with governmental funding in the year 2000, nor was it as easy to drum up support for Bosnia as it had been just after the war. International donors were increasingly concerned by corruption in Bosnia and the misuse of public funds by politicians. So by 2000, foreign donor governments had tightened their purse strings and were insisting on proper financial management, reporting, auditing, and organizational planning. In Boys the ICMP had found the right man for the right job. At first the fledgling ICMP's donors were American, then the Dutch gave funding, and after it became apparent that things were being well run, other foreign donors joined in.[2]

The operational imperatives of the ICMP for Kathryne Bomberger and her team were, by 2000, basically trifurcated. They had to make sure the ICMP could cut across the entities' divides and handle the social and human rights of the relatives; they needed to badger the Bosnian authorities to draft a law to deal with the problem of the missing at a parliamentary level; and, the hardest task, they had to set up a system to identify the human remains that were being exhumed from across the country at the rate of dozens of bodies per week. The critics in the forensic science community were quick to queue up and tell Bomberger that exhuming, finding, and identifying the human remains of the missing persons of Srebrenica would be impossible. Undaunted, the International Commission on Missing Persons picked up the gauntlet. The ICMP's forensic scientists realized that they would have to take the traditional method of identification—using clothing, teeth, identity cards, and personal items—and stand it on its head. But great scientific successes, innovations, and inventions are often a matter of utilizing existing technology and available resources and taking a new approach that, in retrospect, seems simple.

The ICMP's real revolution was in reversing the identification approach. Rather than using traditional, physical evidence to get a presumed identity and only then testing with DNA, the ICMP went straight to DNA and led the process with it. What the ICMP had at its disposal that no other DNA identification facility in the world had was a massive caseload. They were going to be dealing with up to 40,000 potential cases of missing persons across the former Yugoslavia, which included Kosovo, then still part of Serbia.[3] They were able to take blood samples from living relatives of missing persons, extract DNA samples, and compare them with DNA samples taken from human remains exhumed from mass graves. Then the two databases were compared to each other, repeatedly, with ever more accuracy. The number of DNA samples involved allowed them to create an enormous reference database—blood samples could be taken from between one to five living relatives, meaning that the ICMP's staff would be looking at collecting upward of 25,000 blood samples for the missing of Bosnia alone.

Then the next problem raised its expensive, logistical head. Laboratories, particularly ones involving highly trained staff and expensive equipment, have high initial start-up costs, and because they are staff intensive, they also have high operating costs as well. In a normal DNA laboratory, a single highly qualified analyst would follow or perform each step of the identification process, thus making it slow and very expensive. The ICMP introduced a modular assembly-line style of working, more like a car plant, where each technician focused on one particular task, one part of the process, and then passed the sample further down the "production line." This was not just faster, it was also cheaper.

Salaries in Bosnia in 2000 were a fraction of what they were in the rest of Europe: unemployment was astronomical, the country was partly in ruins, and there was an enormous pool of capable junior graduates with good first science degrees who could be employed for just hundreds of dollars per month. And they were massively adaptable. This was to prove to be another of the ICMP's successes, again based upon a seemingly simple premise. From the word go, they employed Balkan staff to work with a Balkan problem in the Balkans. And in Bosnia, this meant mainly Bosnians. Dealing with the thousands of frightened, suspicious, and traumatized relatives of victims—persuading them to give blood samples, explaining their legal and social rights—was infinitely easier when done by one of their own countrymen. The ICMP employed Bosnian staff from the outset; the organization may have had the word "international" in its title, with international senior staff, but the largest percentage of employees were people from the former Yugoslavia, mostly Bosnia.

Bosnians from the older generation could often be set in their ways, traditional, and not particularly innovative or flexible. The best of the younger generation were completely different. They'd come through the war, they'd seen their politicians, their military commanders, and the outside world fail them, and they had learned to stand on their own feet and fend for themselves. They were perfectly prepared for the challenges that the complex mission of the ICMP was going to throw at them. Two of their national characteristics were going to help them. First, a stubborn pride would enable them to endure pitfalls other nationalities would have balked at. Second, humor and a sense of perspective would become extremely important in a job that required staffers to help traumatized war survivors find, identify, and bury the bodies of their murdered relatives.

Bosnian humor could be the subject of a PhD thesis all of its own. To describe it briefly, it is black, self-deprecating, inventive, anarchic, and knowing. This is backed up by an established tradition of gentle rebellion against authority that had seen Yugoslavia develop, for instance, in the eighties and nineties, a rock scene that was equal to the scene in London or New York. For example, in a country where even the cats seemed to smoke, a popular, hard-drinking, louche rock band took a countercultural leap and named themselves Zabrenjeno Pusenje, or "No Smoking."

The comedy programming that came out of Bosnia could well be estimated to compete with established classics like *Monty Python*. Out of the Sarajevo cultural scene in the eighties sprung a cult comedy TV and radio show devised by and featuring a gang of young, clever, urban Sarajevo men, called *Top Lista Nadrealista*, loosely translated as *The Surrealists Hit Parade*. It was wildly prescient in its postmodern knowingness. It featured comedy sketches on air that foresaw the breakup of the former Yugoslavia. One of their more well-known sketches involves a Bosnian family setting up barricades in their apartment and shooting at each other, fingers stabbing at maps, arguing about who has the historical right to occupy which room. The solution to the standoff features the arrival of white-uniformed European peacekeepers. Another questions how, in a future Sarajevo ethnically divided by a wall, separate garbage collection for Muslims and Croats and Serbs would work.

Bosnians were traditionally good at disciplines like mathematics, biology, sciences, and engineering: Yugoslavia had a solidly established science and engineering reputation, and its construction and engineering companies had built bridges, highways, and dams across the Middle East. The rigid knowledge structure of these subjects suited the Yugoslav intellectual temperament. But after the war, the collapse of effective state-level control and the war itself seemed to sap many people of determination.

The traditions and manners and abilities of the hundreds of thousands of good, respectable, and honest Bosnians seemed sometimes to be drowned underneath a tide of corruption and criminality that filled the post-war vacuum. It atomized society. It was not helped by the enormous population shifts that the war caused: the movement of the rural population into urban centers has been a societal constant since the Industrial Revolution, with its attendant woes and fears of the urban, educated middle class coming to terms with the large-scale physical proximity of the rural population. But in Bosnia this movement of populations, and its attendant effects, was made harder by the fact that it was not voluntary, but a forced byproduct of ethnic cleansing.

But science was an absolute that transcended the transience of war. Concrete was concrete, steel was steel, and one plus one equaled two. So for scientists, there were jobs to be had at the ICMP. The job applicants thought the organization was *doing* something. A very commonly used word in the country then was "reconciliation," something that many Bosnians, particularly people like Kada Hotic and relatives of missing persons, felt was either premature or had to be translated into solid actions—actions such as the location and identification of their relatives' bodies; the establishment of reparations, pensions, and social rights; and the ability to possess their husbands' property. They were used to the seemingly empty rhetoric of the international community and hoped the ICMP was different. One phrase used by Bosnians to describe the complex jargon of human rights and democratization so popular among the internationals was to say to the person in question, "*Ti prodajes maglu,*" or "You sell fog."

Science and forensics, exhuming Srebrenica, solving the world's greatest forensic science puzzle—all were as solid as it was possible for actions to be. By the end of 2000, the ICMP could see the way forward, and suddenly everything seemed extraordinarily busy. They took a four-line approach to their work: help create and maintain family associations of relatives of missing persons; build, design, and staff a laboratory system that could incorporate DNA matching systems that were affordable and could handle their enormous caseload; fund their work through international donors and maintain the funding, while deflecting detractors from the Balkans and the international community; and finally, get the identifications right—again and again and again, thousands of times. Of course, given this staggering menu of activities, it would seem obvious that the ICMP wasn't going to be able to please everyone.

First Stop—DNA

Deoxyribonucleic acid, or DNA, the key to human identity and inheritance, is something that everybody nowadays has heard of and, in some cases, understands. It has been made massively accessible by popular science, films, books, and above all, television shows. DNA is the molecule that contains the biological instructions making each species unique. It, along with the instructions it contains, is passed from adult organisms to their offspring during reproduction as the human blueprint that allows inheritance, developmental and evolutionary traits, to be passed along the human reproductive line. It is each person's map of existence, and each map is unique.[4]

A biochemist named Frederich Miescher discovered DNA. He was a partially deaf Swiss medical student who wanted to become an ophthamologist, but his hearing did not allow him to be able to use a stethoscope, which effectively banned him from conventional medicine in the 1860s. While working in the laboratory of Dr. Felix Hoppe-Seyler in Tubingen in 1868, isolating nucleic acids from white blood cells, Miescher began to concentrate on the physiological aspects of the makeup of human blood. While studying blood cells, he succeeded in isolating pure nuclei from leukocytes. He then extracted an acid-insoluble, alkali-soluble, high-phosphorus substance from the nuclei. He called this a nuclein, or nucleic acid—this was DNA.

However, nearly a century passed from that discovery until researchers unraveled the structure of the DNA molecule and realized its central importance to biology. Miescher had argued that his discovery contained the secret of heredity, but nobody could quite figure out why. Scientists in the European academic community, some of them jealous of Miescher's achievements, argued that in fact the work of heredity, as it was known, was performed by strong and complex proteins. The importance of DNA only became clear in 1953 thanks to the work of four extremely bright and diligent Cambridge University researchers—James Watson, Rosalind Franklin, Maurice Wilkins, and Francis Crick—who, by studying X-ray diffraction patterns and building models, figured out the double-helix structure of DNA, a structure that enables it to carry biological information from one generation to the next. Watson, Wilkins, and Crick went on to win the 1962 Nobel Prize in Physiology or Medicine. Franklin did not live to see her work recognized by the prize, as she died of ovarian cancer in 1958, aged 37.

The process of matching two people through comparing repetitive sequences of markers in different sets of human DNA, particularly the sequences called number tandem repeats, or, more precisely, short tandem repeats, is the basis of the most commonly used form of DNA typing or profiling. Scientists compare the information they find at different *loci*, or points on a chromosome—a structure of DNA and proteins found in cells—where a DNA sequence or genome is located. Closely related people—like Kada Hotic and her father or her son—would share very similar short tandem repeat sequences, statistically extremely unlikely to be replicated in any other human being and passed between generations following well-characterized rules of meiotic inheritance that can be detected among relatives. This technique is known as DNA fingerprinting.

The most high-profile use of these fingerprinting methods came in 1992, when a German court requested that DNA fingerprinting be used to establish the identity of SS Captain Doctor Josef Mengele, who was wanted by the Nuremberg war crimes tribunal for his deathly medical experiments carried out in Nazi concentration camps. After being wounded in action on the Eastern Front while serving as a doctor with the SS Wiking Division, Mengele was posted in 1943 as the camp physician to Auschwitz. He was a geneticist, and many of the excruciating and lethal experiments he carried out on Jewish and gypsy patients in Auschwitz focused on heredity, the DNA makeup of zygotic twins, and the condition known as heterochromia, in which the color of each iris in one human being is different. Ironically, it was DNA that led to his identification. A sample was extracted from his femur following the exhumation of his skeleton in 1985 from a grave in a suburb of São Paulo, and, after comparing it to DNA taken from his wife and son, it confirmed his identity to Brazilian investigators.

The ICMP's laboratory staff would be trying to isolate nuclear DNA in the nucleus of each cell from the blood and bone samples. They would then compare the DNA extracted to the database of DNA samples collected from living relatives. A positive identification, or match, was when

DNA base pairs from a sample from an exhumed body could be matched with a sample from a living relative.

It was decided that to make the forensic science and human rights sectors of the ICMP's activities work properly and prove acceptable to all sides of the political and ethnic coin, five laboratory facilities were needed. They were rented or built in the Croatian capital, Zagreb; in Tuzla; in the capital of the Republika Srpska, Banja Luka; in Sarajevo; and in Belgrade. An Identification Coordination Division, which would handle the organization's database, records, and forensic data management system, would be set up in Tuzla. The main laboratory and headquarters were already in Sarajevo, and a mortuary and a forensic reassociation facility specifically for Srebrenica victims would also be built in Tuzla. For handling the very high number of missing persons' remains from the mass killings around Prijedor in northwestern Bosnia in 1992–1993 and from the Krajina, a mortuary was set up in the town of Sanski Most, which lay in the beautiful, rolling countryside of the Una and Sava rivers, in the top left-hand corner of the country. Staff was recruited, facilities arranged, and the protocols of human resources and finance set up; good reporting to the donors was emphasized; and all available information was entered into databases.

The ICMP was now committed to the task of sifting through the pieces of the world's largest forensic puzzle. Thousands of bodies had been exhumed from mass graves in Bosnia, families and relatives of the missing had formed themselves into loose associations, massive campaigns to collect blood samples from the living relatives of missing persons had begun, The Hague Tribunal had continued chasing its suspects, and secondary mass graves were continually being discovered. Everything was happening at once. By the time spring 2001 rolled round and the snow started to melt, it was time for digging season again. Then four things happened in succession that shaped the boundaries and the outline of the puzzle into a much more recognizable and precise shape and changed the Balkans, the ICMP, and the world at large: a new conflict broke out in the Balkans; Slobodan Milošević was arrested and transferred to The Hague; the events of 9/11 occurred in the United States; and, perhaps the least reported, the International Commission on Missing Persons made its first DNA match. The four events were all, ultimately, linked to each other.

Chapter Seven

THE WIND OF CHANGE IN SERBIA

On the night of June 28, 2001, former president Slobodan Milošević was transferred from Belgrade's central prison to stand trial in The Hague on charges including genocide, war crimes, and crimes against humanity committed in Kosovo, Bosnia, and Croatia. On that warm June night, several senior officials in Belgrade, who could sense exactly which way the wind was blowing, called the American and British ambassadors to Belgrade for a meeting and suggested a deal: if the two ambassadors were prepared to arrange for Special Forces teams to come to Belgrade immediately, it could be possible for them to arrest and detain Ratko Mladić, who was reportedly in the Serbian capital that night. The ambassadors were immediately caught in a dilemma. They could easily deploy the teams from among the thousands of troops that NATO had stationed in Kosovo, an hour's flying time to the south, or, if necessary, from Germany or the United Kingdom. But the invitation could be a trap, designed to lure American and British soldiers into a prearranged ambush; at best the NATO troops would be operating inside a hostile city where the only operational intelligence available would be coming from the Serb authorities. Perhaps wisely, they turned down the invitation. The atmosphere in Belgrade was, especially that night, extremely anti-Western. Nationalists and radicals across Serbia were furious that their government had allowed Milošević, seen by many of them as a Serbian hero, to be transferred to the International Criminal Tribunal for the former Yugoslavia.[1] Flying or helicoptering in soldiers from Delta Force or the US Navy's Development Group or Britain's Special Air Service to the capital could have been disastrous.

Milošević had stepped down from the position of president of the Yugoslav Republic—Serbia and Montenegro—in October 2000 following disputed presidential elections. He'd been toppled in a display of popular protest coordinated by the nonviolent civic reform movement called *Otpor*, or "Resistance," which, with thousands of followers from across Serbia, had stormed Belgrade's parliament on October 5, 2000. On the night of March 31, 2001, Serbian special police stormed the villa where the ex-president was holed up in Belgrade, but withdrew after confrontations with the former president's armed guards. Milošević, however, gave himself up and was arrested the following night: members of the reformist-minded government of Prime Minister Zoran Đinđić had brought charges of embezzlement, corruption, and abuse of power against him. The old guard of Serbia, including the army, was furious; the new guard was ecstatic. The West was delighted. Milošević was transferred to Belgrade's central prison, then to The Hague on June 28 via helicopter, where he was placed under the jurisdiction of the International Criminal Tribunal for the former Yugoslavia and thence taken to Holland. June 28 was significant: it was *Vidovdan*, "St. Vitus' Day," which, for Orthodox Serbs, marked remembrance of Saint Lazar and the Holy Serbian Martyrs who had died at the battle of Kosovo Polje in 1389, defeated while defending Serbia against the Ottoman Turks. It was also the anniversary of a huge rally of Serbs in 1989 at the site of the battle at Gazimestan in Kosovo, where Milošević addressed them in a potent nationalist call to arms, seen by many as presaging the Bosnian conflict. It was also the day that the Serb Gavrilo Princip assassinated Archduke Franz Ferdinand in Sarajevo in 1914, which sparked World War I.

One of the results of Milošević's crimes was that the International Commission on Missing Persons was deployed outside of Bosnia for the first time in its existence.

Some of the bodies of Kosovo Albanians killed by Milošević's forces in the southern Serbian province had been exhumed by the Serbs and driven back to Belgrade in an attempt to hide the evidence. Some of these corpses had been buried on land occupied by the Batajnica military barracks on the outskirts of the city. But under the new administration in Serbia, they were to be exhumed.

When the time came to dig them up, the ICMP's forensic staff was called in by the Đinđić-led Serbian government to oversee and assist in the exhumations. A few years before it would have been unthinkable for an international organization with strong American backing to be asked by Belgrade authorities to oversee the forensic exhumation of the victims of war crimes carried out by Serbian paramilitaries. Things seemed to be changing for the better. A reconciliatory worm seemed to be turning. The ICMP was even praised by the Serbian government for their help.

But as Milošević was flown to the Dutch capital from Eagle Air Force base outside Tuzla in Bosnia, sitting aboard a jet from Britain's Royal Air Force, his departure left some of his former protégées badly exposed, mainly Mladić. Milošević's transfer to Holland sent a clear message to the Bosnian Serbs in Bosnia and Herzegovina and Serbs across the Drina River indicted by the ICTY: Serbia was perhaps no longer a safe hideout. Initial international hopes after Milošević's arrest were that Mladić's would shortly follow: the long-awaited judicial payback for the relatives of the victims of Srebrenica and other killings in Bosnia could then begin.

Meanwhile, it had been five years since the mass graves of Srebrenica had been exhumed. Bosnians were furiously impatient: exhumations were continuing at an impressive pace following enormous work, but not identifications. And many mass graves remained to be found. The

ICMP was about to open up its new facilities and had started putting in place their DNA identification methods, but to date, in mid-2001, only 151 remains had been officially identified, and only through traditional means. How much longer, asked Kada Hotic and those like her, would it take?

Hotic had responded to the ICMP as soon as she had heard about their requests for families of the missing to give blood reference samples. As it constructed or finalized its new DNA identification facilities and premises in Sarajevo, Tuzla, Sanski Most, and Banja Luka, the ICMP had launched an enormous request for blood samples. The blood collection campaign was launched in June 2000 and targeted Bosnian families in Bosnia, the western Balkans, European Union countries such as Austria and Germany (which had welcomed hundreds of thousands of Bosnians as refugees), and the United States. One of the largest collection operations in America took place in St. Louis, Missouri. By the end of 2001, shortly after the fall of Milošević, 21,653 samples were taken.[2] Near the end of the campaign in November 2008, 86,662 samples had been gathered.

The blood collection campaign to gather DNA samples paid fast dividends. In 2001, 52 official identifications of Srebrenica victims had been made; after the implementation of DNA-assisted technology in 2002 this number jumped to 518, with 490 more made in 2003, and 523 more in 2004.

The Process of DNA Identification

The ICMP received the blood samples on S&S IsoCode cards, which are rectangles of cardboard little bigger than a cigarette packet. The technicians had simply pricked the tips of the relatives' right index fingers with a fast-firing lancet, or spring-assisted needle, and waited for fifteen to twenty seconds. The resultant drops of blood were then positioned, six in a row, on one IsoCode card per relative, which in turn was then sealed in an air-locked polythene bag. DNA profiles were extracted and then sent to the Identification Coordination Centre in Tuzla. The profiles were then cross-referenced against DNA samples that the ICMP's experts extracted from human remains exhumed from mass graves. By now, everybody was waiting with bated breath to see if the newly devised DNA identification techniques would work as specified. The Forensic Science Division was up and running, having been established by the existing ICMP team, helped by two experienced experts in the field of DNA laboratory systems, one American and one Canadian.

The organization began the identification process by cleaning and grinding all bone and tooth specimens. DNA is protected best inside bones and teeth, the hardest substances in the human anatomy and very often the only ones to survive the biological degradation of time and burial. Bones are made up of proteins and minerals, the two most abundant proteins being collagen and osteocalcin, and the most abundant mineral being hydroxyapatite, a calcium compound of phosphates, carbonates, and fluorides. The minerals act like physical bodyguards to the softer, more vulnerable proteins, keeping out agents or enzymes that could potentially damage the protein. The DNA that is best protected in bone can be found in the osteocytes—a type of cell—of mineralized cortical portions of hard bone, like femurs. So teeth or a piece of bone was used for this. The latter would be extracted from a skeletal element such as a femur using an electric saw, a so-called "bone window" that could be cut from a femur as a sample in profile. This meant that the bone itself did not have to be cut in half, thus destroying further a precious body part, itself already mangled and broken by the burial and reburial process.

The first step in the identification system was at the Coordination Division in Tuzla. Here the samples were verified and the chain-of-custody paperwork checked. Then, in white protective suits and masks, staff ground each bone sample with a handheld electrical device like a large dental drill, scouring the outer surfaces to help reduce contamination, dirt, and other matter gathered in the grave. This was done in a specialized contamination-free facility. Bones also absorb coloring and stains from surrounding earth and from the clothing covering the corpse, and this had to be removed too.

Following scouring, the samples were then bar-coded. Each bone sample was given an identification serial number and entered into the DNA matching system "blind." Staff would have no idea of its identity or its country or region of provenance. Whether it came from Bosnia or Kosovo or another country, it would simply be a human sample of just another human being. The bar-coding would disprove the regular and aggressively fabricated allegations against the ICMP in the former Yugoslavia, where previously warring factions would accuse it of ethnic bias in its identification process, claiming, for instance, it identified Bosnian Muslims ahead of Bosnian Serbs.

Next the samples traveled across northern Bosnia, to the capital of the Republika Srpska, where the ICMP had another laboratory system. Then the samples were washed, dried, put into steel blender cups, and ground down into a fine powder. This process further decontaminated them, making them ideally prepared for the DNA extraction process.

The resulting powdered samples were then transferred on a weekly basis, in padlocked steel cases, to the central DNA laboratory in Sarajevo. From 2000 onward, this was based inside the organization's central headquarters in the area of the city called Ciglane, on the northern edge of the town. All along this conveyor-belt-type process, the sampling and testing process was done in a completely modular way. One person did one thing, and one thing alone. Herein lay the backbone of not just the ICMP's success, but the success of all high-throughput DNA laboratory systems worldwide. This modular approach to DNA typing, with specialized teams for each stage of the extraction and analysis process, was the key.

The Sarajevo laboratory was designed, again, along a modular, conveyor-belt system, and was designed to perform multiple DNA extractions daily. The planned extraction from bone used a specially adapted silica-binding method that ICMP scientists had adopted and devised to result in a high success rate for typing and isolating the nuclear DNA short tandem repeats, or STRs, that the ICMP's staff would be looking for to obtain DNA profiles.

In Sarajevo the samples would be washed and then DNA released into an enzymatic solution and amplified. This involved the extracts being quantified to determine the amount of usable DNA that could be recovered. Often, because the samples would often contain only trace amounts of DNA, processing required the utmost care and expertise to exclude contaminating DNA from sources other than the samples themselves. In the Sarajevo laboratory, all staff would have their DNA profile taken from a blood sample so that in the case of contamination of samples, their DNA could be excluded. One contaminant that had to be removed was humic acid, a constituent part of many soil types, which seeps into skeletons lying in graves. The acid can be an inhibitor to the amplification stage. The powdered sample, now in lysate solution, was then passed through a centrifuge equipped with silica membranes to which the DNA particles adhered. But to find and examine the number repeats the analysts were looking for, the DNA first had to be amplified.

The DNA profile of a person is made by the ICMP using the Nuclear Short Tandem Repeat method. STRs, or number repeats, consist of units of two to thirteen nucleotides repeated hundreds of times in a row on the DNA strand. STR analysis can determine the exact number and pattern of repeating units in a specific region on an individual's nuclear DNA. By comparing the different units, and the numbers of times they repeat on a particular individual's DNA strand, to a database containing other DNA profiles extracted from thousands of bone and blood samples, ICMP's scientists can make a match between two individuals.

Amplification was done using the polymerase chain reaction process. Different regions on the DNA are amplified, with fluorescent primers marking parts of them for visibility. A laser sequencer can then detect the variations in the primed areas, printing out an individual profile of the component parts of the different tandem repeats. Once the DNA is amplified, scientists can reportedly take a DNA profile from as little as a trillionth of a gram of DNA. The resultant profiles were then submitted back to the Identification Coordination Division (ICD) in Tuzla, where the ICMP's fDMS, or Forensic Data Management System, compared them to DNA profiles in its existing database.

The high-tech, laser-driven DNA detection instruments used to reveal DNA profiles cost on the order of $150,000, and a fully equipped DNA laboratory requires innumerable smaller instruments and devices, adding up to huge costs. The ever-watchful and resourceful accountant, Adam Boys, knew that the fledgling organization could save money on equipment like this with a little ingenuity. So, in the very early days, when funds were tight, instead of an expensive medical-grade machine that would stir the DNA samples as they were going through a process of DNA extraction, the ICMP team adapted a chicken rotisserie bought from a local Bosnian market for a $150. They made a lot of things from scratch, too. Instead of buying expensive "glove boxes," large, transparent, rectangular, sterile Perspex boxes used for handling DNA, the ICMP had a company in Tuzla make a serviceable alternative for next to nothing. Technology convergence was roped in, too. Extractor fan technology for laboratories was very expensive but was substantially similar to technology used to extract toxic air from coal mines, again, as used in Tuzla. Their forensic staff proved extremely innovative in finding new and less expensive ways of doing things very well.

With the DNA now extracted from the bone samples, the next step was back in Tuzla at the ICD. This had been set up in the old complex of the town's sports center, all vast glass doors, acres of unused space, and dusty girders climbing to the roof. But it suited the organization well: when it came to finding the ICMP—and widows and relatives of the missing turned up at the door constantly—everybody knew where the sports complex was.

An additional challenge in the forensic science of human identification is the management of large, or in the ICMP's case, vast, amounts of data. In order to handle effectively all the information generated, from grave site recovery to final DNA identification, the ICMP designed and implemented, over a period of years, the integrated Forensic Database Management System, or fDMS. The lowercase "f" was simply a way of branding the system. This was a central, interdisciplinary, and searchable computer database that linked all information related to every grave site reconnaissance, each excavation, all evidence and remains recovery, precise data on all the blood samples collected from relatives, and family reference data. The Skeletal Inventory System for body parts, known as SKIN-V, contained all records of mortuary and anthropological examination, while other databases archived each DNA laboratory process, every DNA profile, each DNA matching of bone profiles to family references, and every DNA match report generated. To say that the ICMP's computer database contained the secrets to many peoples' lives is an understatement.

What they were trying to do was to be summed up by Kathryne Bomberger:

> What we're doing, among other things, is making sure that people cannot say, "This didn't happen," or "These people did not exist." We're identifying people who have been effectively deleted because they belonged to the wrong nationality, religion, race, class, gender, or political group.
>
> I remember an article in the *International Herald Tribune* in the year 2000 [that said], "While mankind has been able to map the human genome, the ICMP is using DNA technology to map a human genocide."[3]

Another Balkans Conflict

Milošević's arrest, meanwhile, had brought the Balkans to the center of the international spotlight. Everybody involved—the populations of four countries, NATO, the United Nations, the European Union, and the international community at large—wanted to know whether the arrest marked a line in the sand for the former Yugoslavia. Would it be possible to turn a new leaf, to start properly reconstructing the shattered countries, shattered societies, and shattered infrastructures across the Balkans now that the ringleader was in international custody? Or was it only a matter of time before fresh conflict broke out?

The answer was not slow in coming. As Winston Churchill had said, "The Balkans have a tendency to produce more history than they can consume." (He was, in fact, paraphrasing an epigram from Saki's "The Jesting of Arlington Stringham" in *The Chronicles of Clovis*, collected in 1911. But the original refers to Crete and not the Balkans.) Meanwhile, while Milošević fell so spectacularly from his nationalist perch, Ratko Mladić welcomed friends and relatives to his house in Belgrade, the ICMP perfected their DNA identification system, and Kada Hotic determinedly tried to discover the whereabouts of her missing relatives, another conflict started in the Balkans. It seemed impossible that after four years of war in Bosnia and Croatia, two years of guerilla war and Serb oppression in Kosovo, and the NATO bombing campaign and then occupancy of Kosovo, there could *be* any more war left to fight. But Kosovo and Macedonia's Albanians thought otherwise. Inside Kosovo, under the eyes of NATO and the UN, the Kosovo Albanian political parties that sprung out of the rebel Kosovo Liberation Army (KLA)— though demilitarized by 2001—had taken power. Hacim Thaçi, one of the former leaders of the KLA, gained control as prime minister and took the southern Serbian province on its road to an eventual declaration of independence.

But while he and his political peers, under the watchful eye of the UN and the EU, were trying to create a new nation-state, Serbs in Kosovo were now on the receiving end of hardline Albanian violence. Some claimed that it was a reverse ethnic cleansing designed to expel part of Kosovo's remaining 100,000-plus Serbs out of the province and back into Serbia proper.

In February 2001 a convoy of coaches crossed into Kosovo, carrying exiled Serbs back to the hometowns and villages they'd been expelled from, so they could visit their relatives' graves. With explosives concealed in a culvert under the road and a command wire, Kosovo Albanians blew one of the coaches up.

At the funerals of the Serb dead a few days later, on the grounds of an Orthodox monastery, one father, his face screwed tight from emotion, took a small, wrapped package out of his wife's bag. It was a pair of children's pajamas, he explained, that he had brought with him so that his two-year-old son, blown to pieces in the explosion, would not be cold in his coffin.[4]

Albanians in neighboring Macedonia, buoyed by the success of their ethnic kin's seizure of power and land in Kosovo, launched a low-scale guerilla war against the country's security forces from December 2000 onward. It was one of the world's first postmodern wars, won before it began, where the reporting of it vastly exceeded its content and process. Massively media oriented, the Albanians, many of whom had fought with the KLA in Kosovo, presented their story, their cause, and their version of events fast and confidently to the world's international media, who descended to cover the West's worst fear: a new Balkan war. The Macedonians, on the other hand, kept the gates of media access slammed shut. The conflict was tiny but intense, and brought with it some 200 casualties, civilian, military, and police; about 170,000 people displaced; one dead British soldier; and some 20-odd missing persons. By the time British paratroopers arrived in the Macedonian capital,

Skopje, on a mission to disarm the Albanian rebels in September 2001, the latter had made a peace deal with the Macedonian state, aided by the EU and America, and were granted many of their territorial and political demands. Across the sun-scorched agricultural slopes of northern Macedonia, where fields of corn grew green, almond trees flourished, and the blue sky in summer seemed huge, there was a sigh of relief.

But then, like a whirlwind, it was as though the Balkans didn't seem to matter anymore, as though a giant hand had pushed it off the map of priorities. This author remembers telephoning a British newspaper with an eager story about two Albanian rebel casualties on a deserted road ready in his notebook, the latest documentation of a decade of Balkans conflict. The newspaper's foreign editor picked up the phone and listened patiently to the subsequent story offering about the two perished Albanian fighters. There was a silence. Then he said, "Not today. Not this week. Not this month. Go and find a television."

The date was September 11, 2001.

Chapter Eight

THE WORLD OF THE MISSING, POST-9/11

As the world reeled, stunned, in the aftermath of the September 11 attacks and the declaration of the war on terror, an almost-unnoticed but vital event took place at the International Commission on Missing Persons' laboratories. In November 2001 they made their first identification using DNA on the remains of a fifteen-year-old boy from Srebrenica. The staff were very satisfied indeed. Suddenly everything seemed to change. The number of identifications rocketed—they made 518 in the next year alone. And the United States dramatically revamped its foreign policy to favor not just intervention in countries like Afghanistan and then Iraq, but also the continuing investment of large sums of money in such intangible factors as post-conflict reconciliation, international justice, and the implementation of hard-hitting and efficacious human rights programs. The ICMP got ticks in all the boxes for these. But the role of the ICMP was going to become more global for a variety of other reasons, too, based not just on human rights but on the specialized high-throughput laboratory system it was developing that could make large numbers of DNA matches on bone samples, many old or "degraded."

The results of the first DNA match were felt immediately by those who stood to benefit most: the living relatives of the dead victims. Kada

Hotic had given her blood sample as soon as she could and had patiently waited for news. She and the Mothers of Srebrenica and Žepa had heard about the identification of the boy from Srebrenica, and this gave them all hope. She had also, naturally, read about the secondary mass graves being exhumed around Srebrenica, and although she had no idea where her husband, son, and brothers were buried, the news of each fresh exhumation gave her new hope. A lot of the bodies exhumed from Srebrenica grave sites had been taken to Tuzla, she knew: her friends and colleagues had visited the new facility that the ICMP had set up there.

On the outskirts of Tuzla, in the car park of the funeral home, there was now a new, purpose-built one-story building that housed the Podrinje Identification Project. This had become one of the two facilities in Tuzla where the human remains of Srebrenica victims exhumed from the dozens of secondary mass graves that littered eastern Bosnia were taken. Kada Hotic knew that there was a horrible chance that her husband, brothers, and son might not all arrive in one piece. Some of her friends had gone to Tuzla to try and identify clothing and personal items exhumed with the bodies: a watch, a comb, the pair of trousers or the sweater they were wearing or carrying when they were taken away. But it had proved futile for many of them—everybody in the mad, horrific last days in the Srebrenica Valley had either carried or worn clothes that belonged to somebody else. Kada didn't want to go to Tuzla and find a pair of shoes that looked like her brother's only to discover that they weren't. A trip there could easily bring unexpected pain and suffering to another family, another relative, another woman like herself. So she waited. And the waiting was the most painful thing. She kept pictures of the family, taken in days when life was normal, when she didn't have to wake up in the mornings, make coffee, and realize her entire family wasn't there.

When breakfast was just a silent absence, she'd make *pita*, the ubiquitous layered phyllo pastry pie so beloved in the Balkans. Sometimes she would find herself putting extra butter between the layers, because her son had loved it like that. And then she'd realize that he wasn't there anymore, and she'd begin to cry.

But the rapid advances in identification techniques suddenly seemed to bring her results. Forensic archaeologists from the ICMP had exhumed a mass grave at Hodžići, a secondary burial site, where victims from the Orahovac execution site had been taken. Kada's husband Sejad was among them.

His body was incomplete. After he had been identified, Kada promised herself that she would somehow find her brothers and her son. Then she left instructions that her husband's body was to be left in the new mortuary at the Podrinje Identification Project until it was time to bury him.

The temperature in the mortuary was set a few degrees above freezing, but it still smelled of decayed life, a musty and sour odor that clung to the nasal passages and hung in clothing. The rows of silver mortuary trays that stretched from floor to ceiling were packed with white body bags. The 876 trays in the aisles were originally built to accommodate one body each, but space requirements meant that many more than that were added to each tray.

Exhumation teams from the ICMP and the two different missing persons commissions from the Republika Srpska and the Federation recovered 1,806 different bodies in 2002 alone.[1] By the following year that number increased, and it increased again in 2003.

Inside Bosnia, NATO troops were arresting war criminals, particularly those connected to Srebrenica. On April 15, 2001, in the eastern town of Kozluk, where Srebrenica victims had been executed on the rubbish heap behind the Vitinka bottling plant, Lieutenant Colonel Dragan Obrenović was out in the garden of his father-in-law's house, according to his wife Bojana. Two vehicles stopped outside the house, and three men and a woman in civilian clothing got out. The men pulled guns and put

Obrenović into the car.[2] The car roared into gear and took off fast on one of the two roads that led out of town back toward the Muslim-Croat Federation. Obrenović knew his time was up. The people in the vehicles were American and NATO personnel, investigators from the ICTY and an interpreter. Obrenović took a last look at Kozluk, and then he and his captors headed to Eagle Air Base outside Tuzla, just over an hour away. As he exited Kozluk, he was no more than a few miles from some of the chains of secondary mass graves that had been dug six years before in the late summer and autumn of 1995. The evidence that these graves had produced, the testimony of those who had survived the killings, the written orders, and the intercepted phone calls were all waiting for him in Holland. Several of his former military colleagues, both subordinates and commanders, would be there as well. Obrenović wondered: had they plea-bargained? Would his former colleagues give evidence against him? Would he be asked to plea bargain? What, crucially, would his son think of the charges brought against his father?

Obrenović had substantial reason for further concern. His former commanding officer, General Radislav Krstić, arrested outside Banja Luka in 1998, had been found guilty of genocide in 2001 and had been sentenced to 46 years in prison. This was the first genocide sentence handed down by The Hague Tribunal—and the third ever since the 1948 Convention on the Prevention and Punishment of the Crime of Genocide. The prosecutors in The Hague seemed to have hard proof: solid evidence, good witnesses, and powerful testimony. Obrenović might have wondered if he would be returning to Zvornik and Kozluk any time soon. At a protest in Zvornik, near the Serbian border, that followed his arrest, one of Obrenović's former soldiers had stressed that his commanding officer had been a "soldier's soldier" who was honorable and had fought the war according to the Geneva Conventions. In a moment of reflection the fighter aired one thought: "Was it just us Serbs that started all this madness?"[3]

Bosnia's International Overseers

The Office of the High Representative (OHR) in Sarajevo, the country's international pro consul mandated to uphold the 1995 Dayton Peace Accords, had a new and muscular occupant by 2003. Lord Paddy Ashdown was a former politician, the leader of the British Liberal Democrats, and a former Special Forces soldier in the 1960s in that country's Special Boat Service, the equivalent of the US Navy SEALs. He then worked for the country's foreign service in Switzerland before entering politics. During the Bosnian war, he was a vocal supporter of effective intervention in Bosnia, and by the time he arrived there he had already given testimony at the trial of Slobodan Milošević. Ashdown had large shoes to fill as the new high representative: his predecessor had been a particularly effective Austrian, Wolfgang Petrisch. It came as no surprise that one of Ashdown's first priorities on arriving in Sarajevo was to devise a strategy to clamp down on the support structures of war criminals. Ashdown might have been a tough, former marine, but he came from a background where responsibly caring for those under his command and in his employ was paramount. He took this approach to Bosnia.

The effective always draw criticism: Ashdown was occasionally taken to task for his seemingly colonial approach to the position of high representative—"Viceroy Paddy" was one nickname—but he was exactly what Bosnia needed at that moment. The world's attention was elsewhere; long gone was the global focus on the Balkans. The Taliban had been toppled in Afghanistan, and a new regime was in place there. Osama bin Laden was now the world's most wanted criminal. The militaries and air forces of the United States and Britain had swept into Iraq that spring: under the auspices of the American Coalition Provisional Authority, forensic exhumations were already taking place of the victims of Saddam Hussein, carried out by the unit tasked with handling regime war crimes. The ICMP, with its strong American backing, could sense that it was only a matter of time, the parlous security situation in Iraq notwithstanding, before the new authorities in the country plucked up the courage to ask for their help.

In terms of justice and reconciliation and dealing with missing persons, countries like Bosnia needed three things: an organization that could find and identify the remains of missing persons, a functioning national and international court system that would find and prosecute war criminals, and laws in place to protect victims and guarantee social, economic, and human rights. And this very same nascent international justice, the simultaneous development of forensic science and post-war reconciliation and the triumph of human rights, went on to have an impact on the current and future nature of conflict, war crimes, and human rights violations and their post-conflict resolution. Following its failure to intervene in Rwanda to halt the 1994 genocide and its humanitarian successes but military failures in Somalia from 1992 to 1993, the international community began to develop responses to complex wars and crises like the one in Bosnia. In tandem, post-conflict responses—justice, reconciliation, human rights, reconstruction—were being formulated. What was happening in Bosnia would shape the international community's responses in places like Kosovo, Iraq, Afghanistan, Libya, and Syria for the next twenty years. And one of these primary responses was the ability to deal effectively with the problem of missing persons.

Political analyst Kurt Bassuener from Clearwater, Florida, moved to Bosnia to work for Ashdown's administration. Bespectacled, engaging, and fiercely bright, he had been working as a political analyst and consultant on Bosnia since 1997, and the Balkans since 1992. He was the son of a US Army intelligence analyst who had been noted for his work choosing the paratroopers' DZ, or drop zone, for Operation Junction City in 1967, the only major airborne operation of the Vietnam War. A highly vocal critic of the international community's failings in Bosnia, though not short on praise for its successes, Bassuener's take on Ashdown's crucial time in Bosnia is simple.

There were two good "High Reps," he says, Wolfgang Petrisch and Paddy Ashdown. Bassuener says their styles were very different, but between 2000 and 2005, the state-building project to bring Bosnia together achieved considerable results. After Croatian president Franjo Tuđman died and Milošević was pushed out, a lot more became possible. Ashdown, says Bassuener, was the most strategic and most political high representative. He wanted to maintain the initiative, and his approach could be summed up by the phrase "if you build it, they will come," by which he believed that eventually the country's political elites would embrace the state institutions, such as the Court of Bosnia and Herzegovina, a united army, a state-level police force, and an intelligence service, that they were compelled to accept.[4]

Once again, for those outside the Balkans post-9/11, with Western troops freshly deployed into Iraq, this all sounded like the routine grinding of post-conflict wheels. However, the Office of the High Representative knew that what it was trying to achieve in 2003 and 2004 would have repercussions not just across the Balkans but in the Middle East as well. Many of the expatriate humanitarians, political consultants, soldiers, and diplomats now struggling to keep their heads above water in post-conflict Iraq had served in Bosnia as well. The state-level institutions that their counterparts back in the Balkans were trying to implement were important to Sarajevo and Bosnia because they were the judicial, administrative, and political cornerstones of a functioning country. The Serbs in the Republika Srpska didn't want them; the Croats in Herzegovina were intent on forming their own third entity; and Bosnian Muslims in Sarajevo were stuck in the middle—they wanted a whole, functioning country but were naturally terrified of any form of dominance by the other two ethnic parties.

In terms of justice, what became obvious to Ashdown on arriving in Bosnia was that the two most high-profile war criminals still at large, Ratko Mladić and Radovan Karadžić, were almost certainly not going to be arrested inside Bosnia. As he put it, it became rapidly apparent that "the avenging angel of international justice" was not going to arrive on some NATO helicopter full of Special Forces landing on an isolated mountaintop to arrest Ratko Mladić. They could not get him by military means alone—his support structure of organized criminals and nationalist politicians needed to be destroyed. Mladić, Ashdown reckoned correctly, was protected by renegade elements of the Serbian security services, and in terms of operational pursuit, Ashdown and his subordinates from the OHR and NATO's peacekeepers were some eighteen months behind him. By the time Ashdown left in 2006, they had got this gap down to a matter of days. The OHR went after Mladić's support structures by running intelligence-led operations with considerable resources, including Special Forces from NATO. They removed 59 different Bosnian Serbs who supported Mladić from positions of power, and thus from their sources of funds.[5] This was not just an example of a clampdown on war criminals; by publicly taking down corrupt, profiteering political figures, Ashdown was demonstrating that such people had no place in a modern Bosnia. For a moment, there seemed to be a glint of hope for the country. Justice, the search for missing persons, clamping down on corruption: things were coming together.

But to the people who had been on the receiving end of Ratko Mladić, it all sounded like hot air. The internationals always seemed to say that they were intent on catching war criminals, particularly Karadžić and Mladić, and nothing seemed to happen. It was clear to Kada Hotic and those like her that Mladić was obviously hiding out in Serbia—very occasionally dashing over into Bosnia—and that Karadžić could be anywhere. But she was impressed by the progress in DNA-assisted identifications. Her husband had been identified, and people she knew had found their missing relatives. One day in 2003 she received a phone call from the ICMP asking her to come to Tuzla. They had found and identified one of her brothers, they said. But there was unfortunately a problem, they explained extremely diplomatically and considerately, given the dreadful circumstances. They hadn't been able to find his head.

And so, after the discovery of her brother's body, in July 2003, her husband, Sejad Hotic, was buried. He had been found in one of the Hodžići mass graves, and as she was to say later, she had left him "resting for two years" in Tuzla before the burial. After the burial of her husband, she left her headless brother Ekrem's remains in the ICMP mortuary, waiting for the day when his complete human remains might be exhumed and put together. This left her still waiting for news about her other brother Mustafa and her son Samir. "There is a place next to my husband waiting for my son, and a place by my brother waiting for my other brother," she said. So, by this point, the remains of half of Kada's male relatives had been found, exhumed, identified, and returned to her for burial. Only her husband had been physically buried by that point. Aside from now searching for her son and other brother, and, most grittily, the head of her brother Ekrem, there was an uncle who was missing too. On the eighth anniversary of the Srebrenica massacre, she, and thousands of other widows like her, went back to the land near the now-deserted former battery factory in Potočari. She was accompanied by some 20,000 mourners, many of them relatives of the 1,600 Srebrenica victims who had, by then, been identified using the ICMP's DNA technology.

The green fields and land across the road from the sprawling warehouse had been dedicated as a huge cemetery for the victims of Srebrenica, known as the Potočari Memorial Centre. On that hot summer day of 2003, she stood as 282 identified victims were buried, their coffins, covered in green cloth, lowered into the ground. The commemoration service was the second official burial at the Potočari site: 600 identified Srebrenica victims had been buried in March of that year.

But for the first time, one of the Republika Srpska's top officials was among the mourners. The prime minister, Dragan Mikerevic, acknowledged that reports detailing the Bosnian Serb military's role at Srebrenica should be taken seriously. He acknowledged to reporters afterward that a crime had indeed been committed there, and that "one needs to learn from one's mistakes, and there have been a lot of mistakes in our history."[6]

There were several thousand police from the Republika Srpska who lined the roads outside the cemetery and were also posted on all satellite roads that spread from Srebrenica north, south, and west. Every 100 meters a police officer with the white, double-headed Serbian eagle on his insignia stood in the shade of a walnut tree, for instance, or on the grassy verge, trying to stay out of the sun. For the Srebrenica survivors who had been bused in from the Muslim-Croat Federation it must have been disturbing: these police officers were here to supposedly represent law and order, movement forward, peace, and stability, but for women like Kada it must have been tempting to wonder what had changed since 1995. Helicopters from NATO clattered overhead; European Union police monitors gathered, slightly distractedly, in their gaggle of different dress uniforms: French, British, German, and Austrian. The presence of the Republika Srpska prime minister at the ceremony was seen as something of a milestone and a significant breakthrough. Kada Hotic wondered whether reconciliation—or *napredak*, "progress, movement forward," as she called it—was on its way. If it was, then the citizens of the Republika Srpska, particularly the more hardline ones, must have been astounded by what happened from November 2003 onward.

Under enormous pressure from Paddy Ashdown, the Republika Srpska government had prepared a report on what had happened at Srebrenica. In a leaked copy of the report first broadcast on a television station in Banja Luka, it was admitted for the first time that Bosnian Serb forces were responsible for the mass killings in Srebrenica. Official propaganda had always denied that any war crimes were committed there, and for many Bosnian Serbs the television report was the first time they had heard that "in the period between 14th and 17th July, a large number of Bosniaks [Bosnian Muslims], captured in Srebrenica, were taken to different locations of Zvornik municipality, where they were detained." The report did not mention the exact number of detainees and did not specify who gave orders for the massacre or how many men were executed. However, it revealed that the code name for the Srebrenica operation was Krivaja 95. Krivaja is a river in central Bosnia. The report named five detention centers where men were held and said that a large number of Bosnian Muslims were executed nearby, their bodies buried in the villages of Petkovici, close to the Drina River dam, Kozluk, Branjevo, and Orahovac.

"There is evidence that the mass graves were dug up and relocated," the report said, confirming what was already well known outside the country. The television station reported that more than 30 civilians, soldiers, and policemen testified about the war crimes in Srebrenica. The investigation was undertaken by the military, police, and intelligence service of the Republika Srpska. The report quoted witnesses who were ordered to remove bodies from makeshift graves to other locations long after the massacre and also said that the orders for relocation came from Colonel Ljubiša Beara, a prominent Bosnian Serb Army officer and aide to Ratko Mladić. Like Mladić, Beara was then in hiding. The Bosnian Serbs were admitting their past actions.

It was a revolutionary statement—imagine Saddam Hussein's former Ba'athist party making a detailed report of his crimes and publishing it in 2003, demanding that he be brought to justice.

In Sarajevo, an international EU military force replaced NATO troops in the country in 2004. Their immediate priority was detaining "persons indicted for war crimes" (PIFWICS). A continuous and focused series of intelligence operations conducted by EU Force, or EUFOR, as the EU's military deployment was known, aimed at finding the war criminals and their support networks. The officer commanding the force was Major General David Leakey, a quietly determined British general with a background in armored warfare who had also been the United Kingdom's military representative at the Dayton Peace Accords. He had also commanded a British brigade of troops inside Bosnia in 1996, so he knew the country, knew the problem, and knew what was wanted of him—results. On only three occasions in fourteen months did he receive credible intelligence in advance concerning a war criminal's movements or presence in Bosnia. He remembers that there was never an occasion where the intelligence was sufficiently specific[7] or detailed enough to allow an operation to be mounted with any certainty of success. Leakey had at his disposal several thousand troops from 26 different nations, mostly European. The military force had no mandate to operate outside of Bosnia, and given that Leakey was convinced that Ratko Mladić and Radovan Karadžić were living and moving inside Serbia, the operational effectiveness of the huge number of soldiers could be strictly limited. The chances of finding Mladić were virtually zero if he was in a neighboring country.

However, the Bosnian Serb general would have been well aware that, in the words of David Leakey, "no stone concerning the possibility of Mladić being traced through networks, including his family, in Bosnia [would be] left unturned." Leakey points out that Mladić's training and experience meant that he was no stranger to the art of terrorism. The most successful concealment is to adopt a credible disguise and limit contact with supporters to either a single conduit—ideally an indirect conduit—and exist in total isolation from associates or to be protected and sustained by a very loyal and close community. Mladić was doing the latter. He would have listened to the news about the government admitting to the events of the genocide around Srebrenica and realized that his days in the house in Košutnjak in Belgrade were a thing of the past. Likewise, there would be no repeat of the night in October 2002 when he was observed dining at the Milosev Konak restaurant in

Belgrade while Carla del Ponte, the ICTY prosecutor, was at a reception at the Swiss embassy nearby.

When Slobodan Milošević was taken to The Hague, Mladić knew that one of the first things that he would do would be to try and deny any command-and-control links with Mladić over Srebrenica. And he was completely right. Giving evidence at Milošević's trial, which began on February 12, 2002, the former NATO Supreme Allied Commander in Europe, American general Wesley Clark, reminded Milošević of a conversation they had had when both of them had been at Dayton during the 1995 peace talks. During the negotiations Clark had asked Milošević: "Mr. President, you say you have so much influence over the Bosnian Serbs, but how is it then, if you have such influence, that you allowed General Mladić to kill all those people in Srebrenica?" Milošević answered: "Well, General Clark…I warned Mladić not to do this, but he didn't listen to me."[8]

While Milošević was still in Belgrade, it was in his interest to be supportive of the nationalist hero Mladić. But now that he was, after all, in a cell in Holland, appearing in court on a variety of war crimes charges, the fear was (though the old guard protested at this) that he could well start selling out his former subordinates in court as fast as he could name them. So Mladić, who had been enjoying life in his house in Belgrade and visiting military barracks across the country, now found himself without his principal ally. A small group of loyal confederates from the Bosnian Serb Army gathered around him. One officer organized a series of people to look after Mladić, renting a set of apartments in Belgrade in which he could hide. The number of people protecting Mladić decreased to about twelve. Mladić had also been formally requested by the ministry of defense of Vojislav Koštunica's government to cease using military barracks and premises as accommodation and lodgings, as he was too easily visible. With Milošević's and the Serbian military's backing receding, Mladić knew that, with his official retirement in 2002, he needed money fast if he was going to continue living, as intelligence agencies would say, while hiding in plain sight. And he knew that the easiest, fastest, and most self-beneficial way to do this was to call upon the sprawling network of criminals (organized and otherwise), former military officers, and politicians in the Bosnian Serb Republic, asking for funds to protect himself, as he now intended to go into semi-official hiding.

For the investigation teams from the International Criminal Tribunal for the former Yugoslavia, Mladić's presumed presence in Serbia made life simultaneously very complex and very simple. If he had been in Bosnia from 2000 onward and the combined might of NATO, Europe, and America's intelligence agencies and the investigatory expertise of the ICTY had failed to find him, it would have been a consummate failure. The ICTY's operational conclusion as 2003 turned into 2004 was that Mladić had been inside Serbia for some considerable time, protected by former members of his military and intelligence apparatus. This made it almost impossible to get at him. First, General Leakey's soldiers had no mandate to cross the Drina River and arrest him, even if he could be found. Second, even if foreign ICTY investigators operating inside Serbia could speak Serbian sufficiently to pass as a Serb—and they couldn't—and infiltrate his network, then it would still be necessary for Mladić's arrest to be carried out by police or military Special Forces teams from the sovereign state of Serbia, unless the government invited foreign special forces in to arrest Mladić. Anything else would be a gross breach of sovereignty. And however much it could have helped in finding Mladić, sending foreign troops uninvited into Serbia in 2004 was, politely put, very firmly not on NATO's agenda. Third, even if Mladić's location were established with sufficient precision, it would mean getting Serbian arrest teams into position without Mladić's bodyguards being tipped off by inside contacts in the military or intelligence or police hierarchies.

So, on a macro level, the onus was on the ICTY to persuade the Serbian government that it was in its interest to give Mladić up to The Hague. This was a job left to the chief prosecutor of the tribunal, Swiss prosecutor Carla del Ponte, and EU member states. Their carrot was hundreds of millions of euros of EU accession funding, and their stick was the economic isolation that would follow if such funding and other development aid to the country were cut off. Carla del Ponte was persistent and bullish, and would travel frequently to Belgrade on a small aircraft loaned to her by the Swiss government, accompanied by her Swiss police bodyguards. Keeping on the tail of Serbia's obligations to cooperate with the ICTY was crucial to the ongoing progress of the hunt for war criminals.

On a micro, and more personal, level, there were a variety of methods that The Hague Tribunal and Western governments could deploy to try to elicit information pertaining to the whereabouts of the wanted suspects. The first, in the case of Mladić, was the $5 million reward offered by the US State Department just after the end of the Bosnian war. The Serbian government had started cooperating with the ICTY, and between 2004 and 2006, it was theoretically possible for them to find and arrest Mladić, as he was being physically protected by a known core network of ten to fifteen people. In 2004, he was reportedly driven to the western edges of Serbia, either on the banks of the Drina, at the border town of Mali Zvornik, or further south outside Visegrad. His target was reportedly the southern Bosnian town of Gacko, in southeastern Herzegovina. Mladić started visiting his cousin Branko in 2001 in the small rural town of Lazarevo, 60 miles northwest of Belgrade, and on one occasion he flaunted his presence, his bodyguards openly displaying their weapons, according to his cousin's neighbor, Nenad Jokovic.[9] So, after crossing the border in 2004, Mladić reportedly on one occasion headed for Han Pijesak and the nearby barracks at Crna Rijeka, which had been his wartime headquarters, and thence to Gacko. He was inside Bosnia for a matter of hours on one particular trip, a few days on another.

The ICTY could not operate efficiently inside Serbia except at a governmental level and through the use of Serbian informers and NATO could not set foot over the Drina, but one small group of people could: the tiny band of international and national journalists based in Belgrade and Sarajevo. One of these was Nerma Jelačić, a Bosnian woman from the eastern town of Visegrad. As the child of a Bosnian Muslim family, she and her family fled their house when a group of Bosnian Serb paramilitaries started attacking and killing the town's Muslims in spring 1992. Jelačić's last memory of Visegrad was of burning houses and of the Serbian regular and irregular troops standing on the town's great bridge, made famous in Ivo Andric's novel *The Bridge over the River Drina*, which won the 1961 Nobel Prize for Literature. Jelačić fled to Serbia, Macedonia, and Slovenia with her mother and brother. Finally they heard of a British headmaster, from a school in the town of Northampton, who had room to shelter six Bosnian families. She was able to become a UK citizen and receive education, and eventually landed a job working for two leading newspapers before returning home to Bosnia in 2003. As she recalled, she wasn't able to help her country in wartime, so she would do it in peace.

Jelačić settled back in Sarajevo. Once there, she bought a small white shih tzu named Dixie that would be her constant companion—the dog was dubbed "the war crimes hound" by Jelačić and her staff. She co-founded the Balkans Investigative Reporting Network (BIRN), which trained the best of local journalists in the business of reporting on international justice, war crimes investigations, and human rights. Her priority was looking, as she said, "relentlessly for war criminals." Beside her desk she kept a wanted poster showing all the head shots of the 30-plus main indictees wanted by the ICTY. As each one was arrested, Jelačić drew prison-cell bars across the culprit's face.

A coalescence of capable and committed people were now gathering to the cause. The hunt for the perpetrators of the Srebrenica massacre, and the solution to the world's greatest forensic science puzzle, had brought a curious and qualified mixture of people on board ship. On the technical side there was the International Commission on Missing Persons, on the judicial side the ICTY and its investigators, and then Nerma Jelačić's lone wolves from BIRN, and a few other foreign correspondents, American and British. One of these foreign correspondents had discovered a Bosnian Serb concentration camp in 1992; another had sworn he'd stay in the Balkans and not join his numerous colleagues in Iraq and Afghanistan until Radovan Karadžić was arrested. As the powerful, reconciliatory human rights *juju* of the ICMP's missing persons program continued, international justice was also moving forward.

Ratko Mladić had long left 117a Blagoja Parovica Street. Nationalist criminals, particularly such high-profile war criminals as Mladić, brought nothing but trouble to the police in early 2005 in Belgrade. The city's mafia had reportedly been outraged, in 2003, by the way at which the popular and populist Western-oriented Prime Minister Đinđić was clamping down on organized crime, cooperating with the ICTY, and transferring to The Hague Serbian army officers indicted for their role in the war in Kosovo. And so organized criminal and ex-military gangs decided to do something about it: in March 2003 a former Special Forces police sniper assassinated Đinđić. The police response was massive.

So began ex-general Ratko Mladić's life on the run. He was set up with contacts, some eleven men and two women, who helped him and arranged for his protection from October 2002 until the end of 2005. He mainly hid in New Belgrade, a sprawling landscape of huge high-rise apartment blocks, many of which were home to people who were not from Belgrade. Mladić settled into the first flat at 24 Ulica Pedje Milosavljevica and then at number 183 Ulica Jurija Gagarina. And once his welcome ran out in these apartments, there was family inside and outside Belgrade. One place for him to hide was just outside the sprawling center of the Serbian capital, in a suburban area that led down to the edges of the Sava River. Rushes grew under the willow trees by this wide stretch of water, just before its confluence with the Danube, and Serbian fishermen went looking for *zander*, or "pike perch," in the dark, bottle-green waters near the small suburb of Mala Moštanica. It was here where Mladić's brother-in-law and extended family had two houses surrounded by woods and a quiet garden, where the former general, now on the run from The Hague for over a decade, could hide.

The Intervention of the Power of Nature

As Ratko Mladić was deciding whether or not to occasionally cross the border between Bosnia and Serbia, looking out of his window in the Belgrade high-rise, as international peacekeepers and administrators across the Balkans were deciding on the most effective way to apprehend him, and as the ship of post-conflict development tossed hither and thither on the Balkans' sea, nature's attention was elsewhere. At two different ends of the planet two different events were about to unfold, not remotely linked to war crimes, human rights abuses, or conflict, that brought the ICMP and its DNA identification system onto the international stage. The first took place the day after Christmas 2004, off the coast of Sumatra. An undersea earthquake, registering over 9.0 on the Richter scale, hit southeast Asia. The earthquake lasted for nearly ten minutes, causing the entire planet to vibrate, and the vibrations caused the seabed to rise, triggering a monumental tsunami. Waves up to 90 feet high hit the coasts of Thailand, Indonesia, India, and Sri Lanka. Some 230,000 people perished. The Thai government turned to the ICMP to help identify some of the victims. The ICMP responded immediately. Each country that had lost people in the disaster sent identification teams to Asia to help with the effort. The ICMP eventually finalized technical agreements in May 2005 with authorities in Thailand on the identification of victims, but by that time they were already analyzing bone samples, an initial 750 of which had been sent to Sarajevo to obtain DNA profiles. For the first time, their software and laboratory system were being deployed to assist the victims of natural disasters, a new process for them, known as Disaster Victim Identification (DVI).

The ICMP deployed staff to Phuket, Thailand, where they established a database of DNA profiles of the missing, and they compared the bone sample DNA profiles they had already obtained with those of the relatives of missing persons, which were collected by the Thai authorities and the authorities of the countries whose citizens were lost. The ICMP's work in identification, particularly of Swedish victims, came to the attention of Interpol, who decided to get involved with them on an operational level.

The crisis in Asia had hardly subsided when Hurricane Katrina began gathering force over the Bahamas on August 23, 2005. It hit the Gulf Coast of the United States and the area around New Orleans. It was the deadliest hurricane in nearly a hundred years, and more than 1,800 people died. The greatest human damage was inflicted in and around New Orleans as flood levees collapsed. The ICMP, once again, saw that the skills they had developed in the Balkans could be deployed for humanitarian ends, and so they wrote to the Federal Emergency Management Agency (FEMA) offering assistance; shortly afterward, the state of Louisiana was in touch and sent bone samples to Sarajevo.

The ICMP used the bone samples to obtain DNA profiles for identification of the bodies and aimed to test 260 to 350 bone samples. Normally the Bosnian laboratories worked with bones from war crime victims, many of whom had been buried in grave sites for more than ten years, making obtaining DNA profiles difficult. But during its more than five years of working with skeletal remains found in mass graves across the former Yugoslavia, the ICMP had perfected methods of obtaining DNA profiles from hard tissue samples. Hurricane Katrina was a relatively recent disaster, and as a result, the quantity of DNA was much higher than in older bones. The combination of hard-won expertise and clear samples meant that the technicians had a success rate of nearly 100 percent. Unlike tsunami cases and those in the former Yugoslavia, the ICMP's involvement in Katrina victim identification efforts was limited to the profiling of bone samples for DNA. The DNA profiles were then returned to Louisiana authorities for matching with family members' profiles there.

Suddenly, the organization was no longer just about Bosnia, the Balkans, or war. The linear development of the ICMP's DNA identification process was now helping human beings in a humanitarian way, a departure from the ICMP's normal human rights and rule of law approach. Swedish tourists on holiday in Thailand and citizens of New Orleans might have seemed a world away from the dead of eastern Bosnia, but when it came to identifying them in the ICMP's DNA laboratory system, all the bone samples would have looked the same. For they were the human remains of, simply put, other human beings.

The International Commission on Missing Persons had very successfully helped, in a very humanitarian and human way, with the aftermath of two of the largest natural disasters in modern history. The world's largest international police association now wanted them on board too. Back home in the former Yugoslavia, the number of positive DNA matches of victims of the Balkans conflicts was increasing. The ICMP's international involvement in the issue of missing persons looked set to increase as well.

At that moment, the end of an era began: on March 11, 2006, Slobodan Milošević was found dead from a heart attack in his cell at the ICTY's detention center outside The Hague.

Chapter Nine

GLOBAL OPERATIONS BEGIN

The bones of the Norwegian SS soldiers took over 65 years to make it from the Russian battlefield north of St. Petersburg to the DNA laboratory in Sarajevo. Russian soldiers killed these Norwegian members of the Waffen-SS Ski-Jaeger Battalion in June 1944, in a pine forest on the Karelian isthmus outside of then-Leningrad. Professor Inge Morild, a Norwegian forensic scientist, took a briefcase containing the soldiers' bone samples, and blood samples collected from their living relatives, mostly grandchildren, to the ICMP's laboratory in summer 2008.[1]

He had turned to the ICMP on advice from a colleague in forensic science and others. The presence of the professor and his strange cargo in the glass-fronted, four-story Sarajevo ICMP office building represented a quadrilineal convergence of the past and the present, between old history and new science, between the technological absolutes of forensics and the variable human emotional fluctuations of loss, memory, and reconciliation.

Even by the standards of the human misery, dazzling forensic achievement, and human idiosyncrasy that is the base currency of the missing persons issue everywhere, the story of the Norwegian SS men was a strange and controversial tale. In 2009 Norway was, in some ways, still struggling to reconcile itself with its role in World War II, when, after seizing power in a German-backed coup d'etat, the government of Vikund Quisling actively collaborated with the German regime of Adolf Hitler. Keen to see Norway out of British or Russian control, Quisling sided with Hitler, thinking the country's best chances of an effective neutrality lay under the Germans. He was proved wrong. The majority of the Norwegian population resisted the Germans heroically: Quisling was shot by a firing squad, on charges including murder and treason, at an Oslo fortress in autumn 1945.

World War II is still sensitive in modern Norway. Sixty years after the end of the conflict, the story of the men who fought and died at the Kaprolat Hills showed how difficult it remained for many countries to come to terms with their recent pasts, and why accounting for missing persons helped quash any potential historical revisionism.

Another European country that had not come to terms with its past, with the problem of missing persons, was Spain. Thousands of persons had gone missing in the era of the Spanish Civil War in the 1930s, and over 70 years later the country was still working out how to deal with the problem.

The point to be made was that it wasn't just countries like Bosnia, or Iraq, or Chile, or those in Central America that wanted or needed to deal with the problem of missing persons: countries like Norway that hadn't seen conflict for nearly 70 years were involved in the process too.

Typically, Norway is considered a small but tough, proud, and determined country. In World War II, as described above, almost everybody resisted the Germans. The story of the men who volunteered to join the SS is the story of those who didn't. In 1940 Hitler ordered Reichsfuhrer Heinrich Himmler to establish a new SS division that united all foreign volunteers into one single unit. On November 1, 1940, he created this SS division under the name "Wiking" and divided it into three regiments: Germania, Westland, and Nordland, with the latter earmarked for the

Norwegian SS volunteers. On January 12, 1941, Prime Minister Quisling asked for volunteers to serve under German command. A total of 291 responded, all of whom were accomplished skiers, making them a natural choice for the Ski-Jaeger Battalion the SS was forming. (The exact number of Norwegians that served in Wiking over the course of the war is unknown, but most estimates put it at 1,000.) At the Hippodromen in Oslo, Himmler officiated at a ceremony where these initial volunteers were welcomed into the ranks of the National Socialist Party's armed protective wing, the Waffen-SS.

Originally, this unit was stationed in Poland, but by July 1941 it was transferred northward as Operation Barbarossa, the invasion of Russia, started.[2] By the summer of 1944, the Ski-Jaeger companies found themselves deployed several hundred miles north of what was then Leningrad.

On June 25, 1941, three companies of the division's Ski-Jaeger Battalion, comprised entirely of ethnic Norwegians, found themselves dug into positions on the edge of a thick forest of pine and ash trees near a lake in the Kaprolat and Hasselmann hills. They were well prepared. They dug trench systems to provide mutually supportive arcs of fire for their MG-42 machine guns and constructed solid bunkers that made extensive use of large amounts of timber from the forest. But when the Russians attacked with an entire motor rifle regiment, half of the Norwegians fought literally to the death, while the other half tried to retreat across the lake behind them, some of them drowning. Their bodies lay where they fell, in the mossy, acidic soil under the pine trees, washed up on the edges of the lake, and in the tufts of strong, wiry Arctic grass, until 2003.

In 2003 and 2005 two groups of Russian and Norwegian historians visited the site and discovered more than a hundred skeletons, along with remnants of SS uniforms, dog tags, moldy leather boots, rusted helmets, gas mask containers, and thousands of brass cartridge cases.[3]

The overgrown defensive positions were also strewn with the remains of Russian soldiers: the Norwegians had clearly put up a stiff fight. The families of the SS soldiers, who by the early years of the twenty-first century consisted of adult grandchildren and more distant relations, wanted the remains of their relatives to be identified and returned to them so that they could be given a proper burial. The Norwegian authorities were not sure; they realized that the country's World War II past was still sensitive. So their initial response to the families of the missing soldiers was to tell them that responsibility for the identification and repatriation of their remains lay with Germany.

However, the families persisted. Finally, in 2007, the Norwegian government provided the sum of 1 million Norwegian kroner—about $170,000—to find, identify, and repatriate the remains of these former SS men. At the University of Bergen a professor of comparative politics, Stein Ugelvik Larsen, formed the Kaprolat Committee to come up with a plan to identify the remains of these Ski-Jaeger Battalion members on behalf of the surviving relatives. Regardless of the allegiances their grandparents had formed in the war, the relatives just wanted to be reunited with the soldiers' remains. They were no different, in many ways, than the relatives of the missing persons of Srebrenica, or Prijedor, or Kosovo, or Croatia.

However, time and repeated exposure to the elements meant that it was going to be hard to extract what DNA remained in the Norwegian bone samples. Fortunately, the ICMP's laboratory was establishing itself as highly competent in extracting small trace elements of DNA from highly degraded remains.

The harder the bone is, the better it is at preserving DNA. (A study carried out by the ICMP's forensic science division in 2007 showed that of 24,656 different skeletal elements tested from human remains exhumed from Bosnia in 1992, Srebrenica in 1995, and Kosovo in 1999, the bones that returned the highest percentage of reportable DNA profiles were the femur, the teeth, the tibia, and the fibula. The femur showed success rates of between 82 and 92 percent.[4]) Therefore, with bones like the Norwegians', the lab needed as many samples as possible. When the Norwegian soldiers were killed, most of the bodies remained in two places: in the moss-covered acidic soil under the pine trees and on the edge of the lake. The majority of the Norwegians' remains were what are known in forensic archaeology as surface remains, meaning they were not buried. The SS men's bones would have frozen and thawed each winter and spring since 1944, adding to their degradation. More importantly, they would have been heavily oxidized—exposed to the open air—and also subjected to "animal interference." In short, Arctic foxes and wolves would have eaten parts of the bodies and bones. As well, the soil on which they had been lying was probably acidic, and after 65 years the effects of even a small excessive balance of alkali or acid in the dark soil would have been enough to help them degrade. Given all of the outside elements that had had an impact on them, it was perhaps a surprise some of them had lasted as long as they had. So, flown to Sarajevo, the bones entered the ICMP's laboratory system.

Proving its ability to extract trace amounts of DNA from highly-degraded samples, the laboratory set to work and, despite the age of the samples they were dealing with, managed to generate 26 DNA reports. Over 60 years after the deaths of the men who had fought in the Arctic forest at the Kaprolat hills, some of their remains were returned to their relatives.

Global Operations

Their DNA profiles were not the only ones marking time in the electronic files of the fDMS, or Forensic Data Management System. Besides the desperate relatives of the missing of Prijedor, Srebrenica, the Krajina, and Kosovo, there were others waiting for the phone call from the International Commission on Missing Persons. In addition to the victims of disappearances, ethnic cleansing, wars, atrocities, and genocide, the database now contained information on victims of natural disasters ranging from earthquakes to hurricanes, from landslides to typhoons.

These were people rich and poor, big and small, powerful and commonplace, who'd happened to be in the wrong place at the wrong time when the hurricane struck, or the rains came in, or the wind shifted, or the gods decided it was time to vent their wrath through the weather or disease or famine or large-scale bad luck.

In June 2008 the 24,000-ton car ferry MV *Princess of the Stars* was traveling from the capital of the Philippines, Manila, to Cebu City, which is the Pacific archipelago's second-largest port. Despite the proximity of Typhoon Frank, the ship was judged large enough to be allowed to set sail. The typhoon was causing enormous waves, gale-force winds, and pounding rains, said the Philippines Coast Guard. But on the morning of June 21, the typhoon changed course, and the *Princess of the Stars* sailed straight into it. At 11:30 in the morning the captain gave orders to abandon ship. A mayday from the ship was received at midday. Radio contact was lost at 12:30. The ship started to tilt and by late afternoon was capsizing.

Access to the lifeboats proved difficult, as some panicked crew members deserted their stations. Some of the passengers were swept straight off the upper decks into the sea. The ferry finally capsized around six o'clock in the evening. Those below deck in cabins drowned as the churned-up waters of the Pacific washed in. The ship turned over and lay sideways, its upper superstructure resting on or near the seabed. The bodies of those swept off the decks were hurled left and right, some discovered washed up on islands hundreds of miles away, where fellow Filipinos buried the bodies in makeshift graves almost immediately. Three days later, on June 24, the coast guard came up with an initial casualty estimate: of the 862 crew and passengers on the manifest, only 48 survived. Sixty-seven were declared dead, while 747 were missing.

The Philippines interior minister didn't have the mobile mortuary facilities, the DNA identification capacity, nor the practiced skills to recover and identify the remains. The Filipino government contacted Ron Noble, the highly-focused American secretary-general of Interpol, at its headquarters in Lyon. Who, asked the minister, did Interpol have on call to help? The answer lay in Sarajevo.

In 2007 the ICMP had signed an agreement with Interpol to provide Disaster Victim Identification capabilities to the organization and the 191 member states it represented. Noble, an American law enforcement official and former undersecretary at the US Department of the Treasury, which included being in charge of the US Secret Service, was in the middle of his second five-year term, having been unanimously reelected by the 74th Interpol General Assembly in Berlin, Germany, in 2005. At his acceptance speech, he hinted at his vision for the world's largest law enforcement organization:

> For Interpol, 11th September was a moment of reckoning. It was time for us to decide what kind of international police organisation we wanted Interpol to be. Although the organization had been created over 80 years ago by police chiefs to provide operational police support internationally, it had become so slow, so unresponsive that in many police circles around the world it had become irrelevant to day-to-day needs. September 11, 2001 changed all that; Interpol went operational, working 24 hours a day, seven days a week, 365 days a year to support NCBs and police services.[5]

The International Commission on Missing Persons was, through its successes at Srebrenica, to become part of this rebirth. In 2008, the organization was still evolving. Indeed, Typhoon Frank marks the first time DNA technology was ever used as the initial method of identification in a highly complicated operation of blood and bone sample collection, coordinated between the Philippines, Interpol's headquarters in Lyons, and the ICMP's laboratory in Bosnia.

Could the organization deploy a team into the Philippines in very short order, Interpol wanted to know. Within hours staffers were packing. What was needed out in the humid Pacific was a blood collection campaign; an ability to take bone samples from the corpses washed ashore, exhumed from temporary graves, or retrieved from the ship; and a mobile mortuary. An analysis of blood and bone samples for cross-referencing for eventual positive DNA matches would be done at the laboratory in Ciglane, with the blood and bone dispatched by FedEx or DHL from the airport at Cebu City. It was not just a question of the ICMP stepping up to the plate, but of Bosnia itself. Interpol wanted an international organization that did as advertised. If the organization happened to be almost 90 percent Bosnian-staffed, based in Sarajevo, and a product of the Balkan wars of the nineties, then so be it. Noble and his staffers in Lyons had signed the agreement with the ICMP because their track record said they could deliver, not just in making DNA matches of victims of incidents like Srebrenica, but in large-scale natural disasters, plane crashes, and terrorist incidents. Cebu City and the *Princess of the Stars* would test this.

Members of the rescue and identification operation worked in some of the most difficult conditions imaginable. As noted earlier, many of those bodies had been washed overboard, but the rescue operation inside the ferry's hull was particularly ghoulish. The Philippines Coast Guard and Navy and US Navy divers struggled to rescue the bodies, in some cases extracting the bloated and dismembered bodies of the drowned victims from cabins inside the upturned hull, underwater, in the dark, trying to maneuver the swollen corpses into body bags as lemon-shark, hagfish, squid, and cuttlefish swam around them. There were two things that further complicated matters: no one knew exactly how many passengers the overcrowded ferry carried, as the official passenger manifest was not reliably accurate. Also, the boat carried 10,000 kilos of Endosulfan as cargo—drums of pesticide for the pineapple-growing industry that were highly toxic. This created an environmental hazard and lethal danger for divers.

The rescue operation went on first for weeks, and then, as the ship's hull lay on its side, half-submerged, the time stretched into months. There were plans to refloat the hull so that a proper examination of the interior could be made by divers. Bodies still turned up on surrounding islands weeks later, and despite the resolute efforts of the divers—none of whom were reported injured—the exact number of people who perished was never exactly quantified. But onshore, what was accurate was the Disaster Victim Identification operation.

The ICMP team, working with Interpol staffers and officials from Cebu City and Manila, collected, in all, some 2,500 blood samples from relatives. Divers pulled approximately 300 bodies from the sea immediately after the typhoon, and 40 of these were almost immediately identified using fingerprints, dental records, and other traditional methods. Some 300 bone and blood samples from victims' bodies were initially shipped to the Sarajevo laboratory for analysis within weeks of the ICMP and Interpol team arrival in Cebu City, and more followed. The recovery team installed refrigerated containers onsite where the victims' remains could be properly stored once they had been recovered from the ferry. Interpol had also shipped a mobile forensic laboratory to Cebu City for the post mortem examinations. By summer 2009, a year later, the team had overseen an operation that had resulted in the provision of positive DNA matches, and thus identifications, of 449 people.

Most of the victims that were found were identified. The Interpol Incident Response Team was almost immediately honored with an award for its "invaluable services" by the Cebu City Regional Disaster Coordinating Council at a special ceremony attended by senior police, disaster management officials, and city authorities on August 12, 2008.[6] "You have contributed greatly in alleviating the sufferings of the Filipino people and uplifted the morale of those in need," the Council stated.

The Typhoon Frank operation in Cebu City was one of two where the ICMP spread its wings. The second instance where the ICMP came to the aid of a foreign government took place in late spring 2008, after the ICMP signed an agreement with Chile "to provide technical assistance in identifying victims of enforced disappearance from the 1970's." According to a press release, the ICMP saw this operation as not only helping Chile achieve "the primary human rights task of helping families and relatives find their loved ones," but also exemplifying "the kind of international professional cooperation that ICMP, as it expands operationally, is prepared to offer worldwide."[7]

Dr. Gloria Ramirez-Donoso, from the Human Rights Programme of the Chilean Justice Ministry's Legal Medical Services, at the signing ceremony asserted that the recovery and identification process provided "a real opportunity for us to achieve justice in our cases."[8] She added that the bone samples delivered for analysis to the ICMP came from a burial site at Calama, a desert region in northern Chile, adding again that more than 3,000 people were believed to have disappeared in Chile subsequent to the 1973 coup.[9] Chile sent 43 bone samples and 73 blood reference samples to the ICMP lab for testing. The Chilean ambassador to Hungary, whose government had signed the agreement with the ICMP, brought to Sarajevo the first bone and blood samples from a war on another continent.

By late summer 2009, inside the ICMP's vast fDMS, scientists were sifting through genetic information from Chile, the Asian tsunami, Hurricane Katrina, Bosnia, Croatia, Serbia, Kosovo, Macedonia, the Philippines, and Cameroon. The DNA profiles themselves were a result of what was called "blind" testing, whereby each bone and blood sample was bar-coded. The only thing that laboratory staff knew about the identity or origin of the material they were working on was that it had a registration number, not that it was necessarily a sample from a particular family of a particular ethnicity or religious group or national background. They knew absolutely nothing about the provenance of the samples they were working on.

The ICTY and the Arrest of Radovan Karadžić

Back in the Balkans, where the expertise to help countries like Chile and the Philippines had been developed, one of the main Bosnian Serb war criminals had finally been arrested. In summer 2009 Radovan Karadžić was sitting in an ICTY cell in The Hague. The former Bosnian Serb president had disappeared across the Drina River into Serbia after the war. On the run for several years, he had taken refuge under the disguise of an alternative faith healer, living in Belgrade under an assumed identity, Dragan Dabić. Some, including a relative, claimed that he had traveled and lived in Croatia under the name Petar Glumac. The latter is questionable. As one of the most wanted men in the world, it is unlikely that he would have chosen a pseudonym where the surname means actor. Or was this a clever way to taunt authority? Karadžić claimed to be an "energy healer" and an expert in what he termed "Human Quantum Energy." He dressed in black, grew a ponytail, and touted alternative cures to rheumatism, impotence, and other ailments. He gave lectures openly in Belgrade in front of audiences of up to 500 people. In the summer of 2008, when he was 63, he was traveling calmly on a bus through Belgrade's suburbs when the police got on the bus and asked him to accompany them. According to Belgrade war crimes prosecutor Vladimir Vuckevic, Karadžić had been happily walking around and living in the city. Was he tracked down by investigators from The Hague and by Belgrade's intelligence services? Was he—as appears most likely—the subject of a tip-off to the authorities in return for the reward money? Was it an accidental discovery by local police? ICTY investigators at the time remained close-lipped, not wanting to compromise their search for Mladić and the other last remaining suspect, still at large, out of the 161 originally indicted since the ICTY began operations. This was a man called Goran Hadžić, indicted for crimes against humanity committed against Croats between 1991 and 1993. By the time Karadžić appeared in the dock at The Hague Tribunal, the folksy faux doctor image had vanished, replaced with the virulent Serb nationalist he truly was. His arrest left Ratko Mladić the most wanted war criminal still at large in the Balkans. Goran Hadžić was still on the run, but 159 Hague indictees had been dealt with and were now in prison, awaiting trial, released, or acquitted, or had finished their sentences or were dead.

Meanwhile the Serb authorities in the Republika Srpska, while admitting that crimes had been committed in eastern Bosnia during the war, rejected the report of the events at Srebrenica that had been released in 2004. The Republika Srpska's prime minister and then president, Milorad Dodik, was a provocative Bosnian Serb of the old school. He played to his electorate and was a consummate politician. The government of the RS frequently criticized the way the missing persons issue was being handled in the country. Although some Bosnian Serb politicians might have persuaded themselves that they were currying favor with their electorate by undermining the work of the ICMP or the state-level organization they had helped create, called the Missing Persons Institute of Bosnia and Herzegovina (MPI), the families of many Bosnian Serbs who had gone missing felt differently. One head of a Bosnian Serb family association said that much of the time they had nothing but praise for the MPI and the International Commission on Missing Persons. They often felt strongly that their cause was being hijacked by politicians. Wasn't it the ICMP, after all, that had gone to enormous trouble to draft the Law on Missing Persons, which would help the relatives of missing persons access their social and economic rights?[10] And wasn't it true that this law was a world first? Many Bosnians were proud of the ICMP, especially because they knew the organization was comprised mostly of their compatriots; only 10 percent of staffers were foreigners.

To understand the behavior of leaders, politicians, and survivors of the wars in Bosnia and Croatia and Kosovo, it's useful to visit the scenes of the crimes. Peoples' behavior makes more sense when one knows what happened to them, and the best place to see this is at the scene of events themselves. Driving across the Krajina region of western Bosnia and the Croatian land abutting it gives a strong picture of what happened there. Even as late as summer 2009, the destruction told a story of Serbs, mainly civilians, expelled from their homes by Croat forces in 1994 and 1995. Olive and pomegranate trees grew wild in the gardens of destroyed stone houses in village after village, their branches pushing through vacant, burned-out window frames. Croat nationalist graffiti defaced doors and walls. Shells of gas stations were left to rust. Schools were chained shut, their windows smashed. The Croat offensive, Operation Storm, had forced nearly 175,000 Serbs from their homes.

In late summer the Krajina is warm and the colors vivid, and the trees and harvests in the fields lend a bucolic air. You can smell the sea, too, and the cobalt dazzle of the Dalmatian coast lies only miles to the south, across the line of low mountains that guard the Adriatic. The physical beauty of the landscape conflicts with the horror of its history. And yet, out of the catastrophic residual human sadness of such places had sprung a subsidiary scientific success. The ICMP would draw on this newfound knowledge to help other peoples, in other lands, some of them no less beautiful than the Balkan countries that lay along and in the shadow of the Dinaric Alps.

Chapter Ten

RULE OF LAW, NOT RULE OF WAR

July 11, 2010, was the fifteenth anniversary of the Srebrenica massacre. In the vivid green grass of the Potočari Memorial Centre, another 775 DNA-identified victims were buried, a small fraction of the 6,481 victims of Srebrenica that had so far been identified by the International Commission on Missing Persons since they'd made the first DNA match back in 2001. The anniversary proceeded, as it did each year, with speeches, a massive crowd, the normal sweltering summer weather, sometimes overlaid with thunder and rain, and the dignified, painstaking procedure of the burial of the bodies that had been identified over the preceding year. The bodies had been driven to Srebrenica two or three days prior to the ceremony in a slow convoy, and in each town and village they passed through, particularly in the Federation territory of Bosnia, people would line the streets in silence to watch them pass, sometimes running up to the lorries to press a flower or two into the tarpaulins of the vehicles.

Based upon the number of persons reported missing, the ICMP was using a baseline figure of 8,100 people missing following the fall of Srebrenica. This was lower by a couple of hundred than the number on the official memorial stone at Potočari, higher than the number agreed upon by the Republika Srpska government in their 2004 report, and substantially higher than many more of the revisionist and disput-ing accounts. Arguments had ricocheted back and forth for years about how many people had died, gone missing, or been taken prisoner. In *Popovic et al.*, the case that came before the ICTY in 2010 that involved five different Srebrenica defendants, the prosecution had submitted that the number of men alleged to have been killed following the fall of Srebrenica stood at 7,826.

In the years following 1995 the relatives of thousands of the people reported missing had given blood samples. The enormous exhumation work on primary and secondary mass graves had turned up bone sam-ples that had allowed thousands of matches to be made with these blood samples, resulting in 6,481 Srebrenica identifications by July 11, 2010.

There remained bone samples that had yielded individual DNA pro-files but had not found a match—the number of people missing and the number of individuals' remains exhumed and recovered was thus greater than the number of people for whom individual DNA match reports had been issued, or, in other words, identified.

By the end of July 2010, the ICMP had made a total of 13,135 iden-tifications of persons missing from Bosnia and Herzegovina during the war—Srebrenica included—based upon the number of these successful DNA matches. It had collected a staggering 69,922 blood samples from relatives of victims for Bosnia alone and analyzed 28,826 bone samples.[1] To the delight of those who had been there at the beginning, the orga-nization had been branded "a global centre of excellence"[2] by British foreign secretary David Miliband on his visit to Sarajevo. Professor Niels Morling, president of the International Society for Forensic Genetics in Copenhagen, had said that "their work done with DNA is, without doubt, the single most important achievement within the field of human identification with DNA."[3]

After the annual commemorative ceremony had been finished, the bodies buried, the busloads of family associations returned to their hometowns, it was time for the long drive back to Sarajevo through the scorching summer sun, past the policemen of the Republika Srpska deployed every hundred meters in the shade on the side of the road, and Sarajevo's silent bars and restaurants—in keeping with the traditions of July 11, little or no music was played in the city's establishments.

The following day, Adam Boys, in a blue city shirt with sleeves rolled up, shod in brogues, leaned back in his swivel chair at the ICMP headquarters, wiped his glasses on the front of his shirt, and stared out of the window at the graveyards below, reflecting on the events of the previous day. When it came to Srebrenica, it was absolutely vital to get the figures right, he said. The provision of evidence to war crimes trials was not among the ICMP's primary mandated objectives, but, among other things, the organization was very much in the business of accounting accurately for those who went missing in countries like Bosnia. The huge and disputed numbers of predominantly Serb and Roma persons killed at the concentration camp of Jasenovac in Croatia in World War II could be said to have been one of many factors that had fueled the last Bosnian war. The ICMP, he said, had by now steered the grief of family associations into an ability to hold governments accountable, and focusing on missing persons was the first way of normalizing relations between states. It was, he said, the rule of law versus the rule of war.

But by specific request, the ICMP did provide evidence to trials going on in The Hague. On Boys's desk was an e-mail from the prosecutor's office of the ICTY, asking if the organization would be able to provide material evidence in the trial of former general Zdravko Tolimir, one of Mladić's key associates.[4] The ICMP had already received requests from both the defense and prosecution to provide evidence in the case against Radovan Karadžić. Boys added that it was likely they would receive another request if and when Mladić was arrested. If the families of missing persons were prepared to allow DNA match reports pertaining to their missing relatives to be used as evidence, then the ICMP were happy to facilitate this. But the final decision rested with the families.

Boys's desk was full, and the organization was busy. Staff had returned from the American Academy of Forensic Science's annual meeting in Seattle, where they had presented the ICMP's Forensic Data Management System. The Peruvian authorities had been in touch with the DNA laboratory asking the ICMP to help them with processing some samples from families who had missing relatives. Two new grave sites had been unearthed in Chile. In the pile of papers by Boys's computer was the new application for funding for their advisory mission to the Colombian government. Then the Turkish embassy in Sarajevo announced it would donate more funding to the organization, making it the eighteenth international government to do so. At the same time, annual and quarterly auditing was coming up. The Danes wanted the ICMP to help advise them on a "Mass Fatality Plan" (MFP), a legal and insurance-led dictate to be deployed in Copenhagen for the forthcoming Climate Change Conference, put in place should the massive venue collapse or catch fire or be blown up.

Meanwhile, Iraqi forensic scientists, representatives of the largest ongoing project of all, were arriving shortly to look at the ICMP's laboratory system. With estimates of missing persons in Iraq, not just from Saddam Hussein's regime and the two Gulf Wars, but also from the Iran–Iraq war, standing at anywhere between 350,000 and 1.5 million, the Iraqi government had suddenly realized that it desperately needed help if it was going to address the issue. Kathryne Bomberger had already addressed the UK parliament about this, and ICMP training teams had been cautiously deployed into Baghdad and Erbil on advisory and assessment missions. The Americans, seeing how their funding of the ICMP's operations in the Balkans had borne such results, were prepared to fund the mission. In the immediate aftermath of the fall of Saddam Hussein in April 2003, initial forensic investigations in Iraq were handled by American teams from the US Army Corps of Engineers, with various experts attached. They were concentrating on what were termed "regime war crimes," or those committed under Hussein's rule.

When they departed, Iraqis and Kurds were left desperate to find out what happened to thousands of missing persons kidnapped, blown up, shot, forcibly disappeared by Saddam's death squads, vanished during the war with Iran, or executed by gunmen of different sects during the insurgency. Over 112,000 civilians were estimated to have died from 2003 to 2012 alone.[5] The number of missing persons in Iraq, in truth, ranged enormously according to different public sources.

In addition, the Medico-Legal Institute in Baghdad had reported that it had been receiving an average of 800 bodies per month since 2003 and was unable to identify a significant proportion of these. Iraqis would bring in dead bodies, often mangled and mutilated, sometimes bearing marks of torture, wrapped up in carpets and transported on the roofs of cars or in the beds of pickup trucks. These were the victims of the postwar insurgency, and they would sit in the overcrowded mortuary until someone came in to identify them. There was no workable DNA identification facility, no organized blood collection campaign, and family associations were ragtag groups of well-meaning women desperate for outside help.

So, using its experience from the Balkans, the ICMP deployed forensic experts to train Iraqi staff, as well as experts from their Civil Society Initiative section. These were drop-in, experienced human rights troubleshooters, women and men who could get associations of family members of missing persons organized, who could deal with government officials, and who could work in the extraordinarily bureaucratic but constantly shifting operational environment of a post-conflict Middle Eastern country.

The forensic training programs took place amid the security lockdown of the hot, dusty compounds of fortified villas in Baghdad. The

ICMP teams were watched over by British and Fijian and Nepalese ex-soldiers, toting Swiss assault rifles, men who had learned their trade in the British Army in Kosovo or Sierra Leone or Afghanistan. In Erbil, Kurdistan, another training site, security was less stringent and movements more relaxed.

Plastic skeletons were buried in the sandy soil of the ICMP compound to simulate a mass grave site, and trainees would practice exhumations. Then, when the trainees were ready to deal with the real thing, they would head out in the scorching heat in an armed security convoy to a dusty, windblown mass grave that could be anywhere in Iraq and could contain Sunnis, Shias, or Kurds.

Despite ongoing problems and security concerns, and before the arrival of the ICMP, the Iraqi government had actually taken real steps in the postwar conflict of Baghdad to address the issue of missing persons. These included issuing a decree back in February 2005 to create a National Centre for Missing and Disappeared Persons and drafting the Law on Missing Persons and the Law on Protection of Mass Graves, which had already been approved by the National Assembly. From 2004 onward the ICMP had been able to provide what they politely called "limited assistance" to the Iraqi government through the Ministry for Human Rights to address the problem of missing persons. This had included the formulation of policy initiatives to address the needs of the families of the missing, to create a technical plan to locate, recover, and identify victims, and to build the institutional and legal capacity necessary to house this process. In addition, in such time as they could deploy, the ICMP would provide training for staff members of the Medico-Legal Institute and the Ministry for Human Rights. It had already hosted exchange visits of family association members, as well as visits by the Minister for Human Rights and the staff of the Office of the Prime Minister to ICMP facilities in Sarajevo. And then, by 2009, the

ICMP mission in Iraq was up and running, with its personnel on the ground in Baghdad and Erbil.

The Americans and the British, highly mindful of the human rights and forensic efficacy of the ICMP's programs in the Western Balkans, provided funding for the program. The training for Iraqi ministry staff stressed the legal side of the work by providing Iraqi staff members with the ability to conduct site assessments and to properly record mass grave sites. The so-called Law on the Protection of Mass Graves prevented Iraqi families from digging up burial sites to look for their individual family members, something that had happened frequently prior to the implementation of legislation. The ICMP had also provided the Iraqi government with a proposal to identify the large number of unidentified mortal remains in the custody of the overcrowded mortuaries.

Security in Baghdad, particularly, was sometimes less than ideal. On one mission into the center of the Iraqi capital, a convoy of three armored vehicles containing ICMP staff members missed an exploding roadside bomb on a highway interchange by only 30 meters. In June 2012, 107 people died in bombings and shootings in and around Baghdad. Unfortunately, the continued fighting in Iraq and perilous security situation limited the scope for helping the country address the issue of missing persons.

The View from Bosnia of the Rest of the World

The ICMP had been based in a plain tinted glass–front office, four stories high, in the Ciglane suburb of Sarajevo since 2000. Outside its doors hummed the daily activity of the city fourteen years after the end of the Bosnian wars.

Across the road stood three of the vast cemeteries, with their acreages of graves, that sprawled across the capital, and nearby was a ramshackle market that stretched out under a large highway overpass bridge. Here, everything and anything was for sale: glistening, bronze-scaled carp and *klen,* a cross between chub and barbel, were laid out on pages of newspaper in front of the old men who'd just caught them in the green waters of the River Bosna up the road. Market stalls stood stacked in spring and summer with everything from raspberries to parsnips to red peppers to yellow new potatoes. Next door were butchers' shops where whole sheep carcasses hung suspended upside down, gluey, coagulating blood dribbling in tendrils from nostrils and eyes. Their dead eyes lay glazed on the groups of Bosnian men playing chess in front of the market stalls, Drina cigarettes in nicotine-stained hands, shot glasses of homemade *rakiya* brandy helping the game along. Squat Roma women with tattooed hands in muddy plastic shoes crouched in front of huge piles of cheap cotton underwear, shrill voices crying "*Gajcice, gajcice*" ("Knickers, knickers") every 30 seconds. Next to the stalls manned by head-scarved Bosnian grandmothers selling piles of hens' eggs in six different sizes were the tables of pirated DVDs, some of them pirated copies of pirated copies. Every taste was catered to: *Inglourious Basterds, Avatar, Sherlock Holmes, Ice Age 3, Call of Duty: Monte Cassino,* along with a substantial array in dusty plastic cases of such titles as *Backdoor Convent* and *Gang Bang Gladiators.*

Meanwhile, on the fringes of the market, people sold their possessions simply to live: old pairs of shoes, a bicycle pump, a worn leather coat, and hundreds of old Yugoslav-era school textbooks and handbooks about communism.

Inside the plain ICMP building, however, behind the drab exterior, lay the front line of investigative forensic science, real-life *CSI* in action.

In the ICMP headquarters, two floors below Boys's office, bone samples from countries outside the Balkans were now being processed by the laboratory system. There was a new addition to the laboratory too. The German pharmaceuticals manufacturer Qiagen, who supplied some of the organization's chemicals, had devised a robotic device for helping in the extraction of DNA samples. Staff in the laboratory had named it "Awesomo" after the robot that Cartman builds in *South Park*.

Next door to Adam Boys's office was Kathryne Bomberger's. By 2010 she was in her sixth year as director general of the ICMP. By her desk was an elaborately lettered certificate from the French government from 2007, in which it was declared that Bomberger had been made a Chevalier de La Legion d'Honneur, in appreciation of her work done with missing persons. For an American, this was quite rare, an honor that put her in the company of Pamela Harriman, Dwight D. Eisenhower, and Miles Davis.

As Boys sat next door working on nine things at once, Bomberger was dealing with details of ICMP operations with Interpol. The ICMP's latest mission with them had been an assessment trip to earthquake-stricken Haiti earlier that year. Then there had been a meeting in March at Interpol's headquarters in Lyons, where a new agreement on the provision of Disaster Victim Identification skills had been reached.

Other issues were coming up as well. Filming had begun for *Belvedere*, a Bosnian-made feature film centered around the story of one Bosnian woman looking for missing relatives, and a team of Bomberger's staff had assisted the filmmakers with constructing a simulated mass grave. While filming had been going on, a Bosnian woman had mistaken the set for an actual grave site and inquired as to whether there might be news of her disappeared offspring. The lines between life and art were becoming more and more blurred.

Meanwhile, the ICMP wanted to establish a new international headquarters, preferably in a major European city where they could be closer to other international organizations, and from where major interventions and deployments abroad could be organized more easily than from Sarajevo. Geneva, Brussels, and The Hague had all been mooted, and discussions were ongoing.

Bosnians Bury and Rebury Their Relatives

As they considered their geographical future, the ICMP's core work was continuing. In their fDMS, the details of Kada Hotic and her relatives could be found. In 2010, the complicated exhumation, identification, and burial procedures of her family were continuing. Both of her brothers, Ekrem and Mustafa, had been exhumed and identified, as well as her husband Sejad. The latter, and brother Ekrem, had been buried in the Potočari Memorial Centre. The remains of Mustafa's head had not been found, so he was awaiting burial in the mortuary at Tuzla. The dilemma she faced, of searching for parts of her relatives' bodies before they could be buried, was horribly common.

Mothers, sisters, and daughters might receive a phone call telling them that a new mass grave had been exhumed and DNA samples taken from the human remains that had been discovered. They would be told that parts of their sons or husbands or brothers had now been identified.

The relatives would then decide what amount of bones formed enough of a percentage of the body to warrant burial. That year, agreements had just been reached with family associations that 466 of the still-incomplete but identified bodies on the shelves of the Podrinje Identification Project would be buried.

Some of those relatives of missing persons were adamant that nothing but a nearly full skeleton was good enough; they refused to prepare a burial with only one bone. Hotic was, by this time, the deputy president of the Mothers of the Enclaves of Srebrenica and Žepa. The president of the organization was Munira Subasic, a determined and forceful woman from Srebrenica whose focus was keeping the plight of the missing and their surviving relatives on the country's and the world's human rights agenda. Subasic's forcefulness made her one of the best possible people to keep an issue like Srebrenica and the missing persons of Bosnia in the national and international spotlight, regardless of what else was happening. She and the staff at the ICMP had formed a mutually under-standing and productive relationship. Not a single regional conference on missing persons, nor a key parliamentary meeting, political hearing, or prominent newspaper article or television segment seemed to occur without Munira and the Mothers' presence. In 2010 she had suggested that Kathryne Bomberger and the entire ICMP be nominated for the Nobel Peace Prize. She was one of those people who would carry the torch of the cause ceaselessly—if it showed signs of going out, she'd relight it immediately. In the confrontational climate of the Balkans, where being strong, making noise, and not giving in were seen as the way to do things, she was the perfect person for the job.

But her critics—and there were many, particularly in the Republika Srpska—criticized her because she was pushy and because her priority seemed to be the Srebrenica victims. Ironically, this critique was actually true; many believed that she wouldn't have had to focus on Srebrenica if the Bosnian politicians had dealt with the matter properly. If the politi-cians had done their jobs, she wouldn't have had to spend all her waking hours pressuring other people to deal with the situation.

There were other mothers of missing persons in countries with similar problems: in Guatemala, Russia, Chile, Argentina, they were des-perate for results and tried to get their governments to deal with the problem, even on the not-infrequent occasions when the government and the perpetrators were linked. Being a mother of the missing was a calling that required courage and determination.

Subasic was not alone in possessing these qualities. Bosnians wanted to put the past behind them, and discussing the events of the war was one way of doing this. Many Bosnians traveled widely, having an enor-mous diaspora abroad. They had endured, survived, and, in some cases, triumphed, by surviving a war that would have brought many other civ-ilized countries to their knees. Imagine if the Bosnian war had happened in northern Europe or America or Asia, said some analysts. Imagine people in France, Japan, or the United States in 1995, months after a full-scale civil war, being urged by a vast peacekeeping mission, mainly staffed by aid workers and soldiers from African and South American countries, to embrace reconciliation and commit to democratic best practice. Would their populations have reacted any more positively than the Bosnians?

Those who fight and survive wars, and specifically those who lose them, can be convinced the experience sets them somehow apart from the rest of the world. A kind of instinctive self-protection is one of the psychological mechanisms that allows identity and pride to survive in the face of otherwise overwhelming defeat. This was certainly true in the Balkans. For some of the more unfortunate Bosnians after the war, pride and an admirable refusal to give up was all they had left. There were flashes of solipsism, self-regarding obduracy, and an enduring stubbornness to the national psyche, but the upsides of the Bosnian character—bravery, vast humor, loyalty, a wry, experiential intelligence, generosity, an anarchic sense of fun—showed through very quickly. Sometimes it seemed as though the international community and the outside world had much to learn from Bosnia, not the other way round.

Before considering what Hotic, Subasic, and hundreds like them decided to do with the exhumed, partial remains of their relatives, it must be stressed that what these women—and they were almost all women—had been fighting for were the body parts of their men. That was their main priority. They wanted some physical remains that they could properly bury and that would allow them to remember and believe that those close to them had actually existed, that the Bosnian Serb campaign of ethnic cleansing or the executions in July 1995 hadn't simply eradicated their husbands, sons, and brothers from human existence. As Adam Boys said, it wasn't just a matter of forensic science: it was an urgent matter of human beings, human identity, and human rights. The ICMP was returning the remains to the families and was effectively giving the bodies back their human identities. They were saying to the families, "Your son, your father, the person you loved, *did* exist."[6]

The families also wanted visible, effective justice, something they felt had perpetually eluded them. Specifically, they were frustrated by the respective authorities' seeming inability to arrest Ratko Mladić and try Radovan Karadžić faster. In addition, they often wanted some form of compensation, either money or an admittance of responsibility and guilt from international parties such as the Dutch government and the United Nations. In April 2002, the entire Dutch cabinet, under then–Labour prime minister Wim Kok, resigned just a month prior to general elections in the country. The mass resignation was spurred by the publication the month before of a report by the Netherlands Institute for War Documentation that blamed the Dutch government and cabinet for many of the events surrounding and leading up to the Srebrenica killings. The Dutch queen Beatrice accepted the resignations of the ministers and appointed a caretaker government until general elections in May of that year.

A number of the Mothers of Srebrenica and Žepa, Hotic included, had brought legal action, seeking compensation, against the Dutch government in 2006. Nusan Husanović, a Srebrenica survivor, had taken a separate case against the Dutch state along with two other plaintiffs.

The survivors of Srebrenica wanted to believe that what had happened to them would not happen to others, and they wanted reconciliation. Not with the triggermen from the Skorpions or the Drina Wolves or the VRS 10th Sabotage Detachment, but reconciliation that could enable them to live with themselves and their pasts.[7] By giving them back the whole or partial physical remains of their relatives, properly identified, the ICMP had performed a major act of reconciliation; it meant that the grieving widows had a physical object, something that had been forcibly and illegally taken away from them, that was now considerately and, above all, legally returned as *their* property.

A visit to Hotic in May 2010 exemplified this. She was sitting in the office of the Mothers of Srebrenica and Žepa, looking at photographs of her children and male relatives. In photographs, of course, everybody always seems to look younger; like in memory, people are fixed in time, in that forever moment when we last saw them. And so it was for Hotic. It had been fifteen years since the 65-year-old Bosnian Muslim widow last saw her son, husband, two brothers, and uncle alive, and as she looked at their passport-sized photographs spread in her open hands, the memories coursed back like an electric current of absence and loss.

She sat in a ground-floor office set in a towering old Yugoslav apartment block in the Cengic Vila area of Sarajevo. Outside it was drizzling, a little cold, and although the green cacophony of a southern European spring was exploding on the chestnut and lime trees on the central boulevard outside the office window, the temperature was uncharacteristically chilly for May in Bosnia. So Kada shivered slightly as she poured strong black Turkish coffee into small white cups, the beads on her amber-colored necklace clicking slightly as she leaned over. The office was newly decorated and smelled heavily of emulsion paint. The walls behind her bore photographic testimony to what had happened on those blazingly hot afternoons in July 1995, and to what she and thousands of other mothers and wives of Srebrenica had had to go through. There were hundreds of pictures of her and other members of the association at meetings, conferences, and rallies, with Queen Noor of Jordan, Bob Dole, and Kofi Annan. She had pinned up t-shirts with the logo "Srebrenica Genocide 1995" on them. Another was emblazoned with a map of Bosnia with different massacre sites pinpointed in red, yellow, and blue spots.

She exhaled, not quite a sigh, and looked out of the window. When her husband's body was exhumed, he'd had a silver pocket watch in his trouser pocket. It had stopped at 4:30 pm, after being hit by a bullet. By summer 2010 she was the vice president of the Mothers of Srebrenica and Žepa. For Hotic, the answer to the question of what the ICMP gave her, in terms of reconciliation, was simple: "ICMP did great things for us," she said, pouring more coffee. "They found the ones we love."[8]

But the finding was nothing if not painful. Until the body of her brother Mustafa was complete and that of her son found and identified, Kada wasn't going to bury them. Hundreds of other mothers were in the same situation.

One of them was Habiba Masic, whose husband and two children had been killed at Srebrenica. She had given a blood sample to the ICMP, who had then subsequently telephoned her to say that following a successful exhumation they had found up to 90 percent of her husband's body. The problem was that the body had been dispersed among four different mass graves: a leg here, two arms there, a pulpy, crushed rib cage with bullet holes in the third, a head in the fourth. A small part of one of her sons had been found, but the identification techniques could not yet tell exactly which son it was. She said she could not bury the precious fragment, for what would the gravestone say? Sadem Masic, 1976–1995? Or Sadmir Masic, 1977–1995? Brother was now waiting for brother, she was to say at the time, in an interview with Aida Čerkez-Robinson, a Bosnian journalist from the Associated Press who by 2009 had been covering her country for eighteen years. Titled "How Many Times Can You Bury Your Child before You Go Mad?" it was the only article about the ICMP that reduced the level-headed and tenacious director general, Kathryne Bomberger, to tears. Čerkez-Robinson wrote:

> It is hard to imagine anybody would envy [Masic], but Rufeida Buhic, 68, does. Her husband was killed early in the war. Serbs caught her only son, Razim, 17, when he tried to escape from Potočari. A massacre survivor told her Razim was one of the first to be shot. His body was never found. Mrs. Buhic returned to her prewar home near Srebrenica to be where the three had lived together. "That's where they walked, where they worked. That's where I want to walk," she said. When neighbors see her working

around the house and the garden all day, "They say, you really work too much. But I'm not alone, I tell them. The two are with me and are helping me." Mrs. Buhic can't sleep at night. No medication helps. Often she visits a neighbor's house, where her son's friend lived and where Razim once measured how tall he grew. She goes there just to look at the line carved in the wood of the doorway: 195 centimeters, or nearly 6 ft 5 ins. Constantly, she checks her mobile phone.

"Every time it rings, I think they are calling me to say they found him...even one bone," she said.[9]

Real-Life CSI

One summer recently, driving through the August heat on an assessment visit to the ICMP's facilities in northeastern Bosnia, a European political visitor made a revealing comment. She was looking at the drab, flaking paint on the worn-out Tuzla sports stadium where the Identification Coordination Division was based, and where the first refugees from Srebrenica had arrived in Tuzla in July 1995. Sitting in one of the ICMP's dark blue Ford estate cars piloted effortlessly by one of the organization's drivers, she looked at the building and remarked that this was not what she had expected at all. She came from a highly developed European political economy, and here she was, discovering, much to her surprise, that the world's leader in DNA identification did not operate out of big, shiny offices and an environment where everything worked faultlessly. She realized what Bosnia was like, and how the triumphs of flexibility, making do, cutting corners, pushing the envelope, guessing the cards, and keeping one step ahead were needed to succeed. And how hard the ICMP had had to work to get where they had. This wasn't like Austria or Germany or Switzerland, she said, as the reality started to sink in. But the whole point, of course, was that Bosnia and Herzegovina *wasn't* a country with a stable recent history, an affluent population, and, above all, a secure political economy. Just over a decade before, Bosnia had been through the worst conflict in Europe since the Red Army and the SS Wiking Division had clashed on the Danube in Operation Konrad at the beginning of 1945.

Despite what the general public might have been led to believe about the world of investigative forensic science by such television series as *CSI*, the ICMP's various facilities in Bosnia looked remarkably pedestrian and low key. Nothing was flashy, and everything was practical. This world was not the world of a shiny, Miami-based, purpose-built headquarters full of slick young professionals in ironed chinos and button-down shirts, traveling by sleek silver Humvees. This was not a world where flashlights with blue beams, rapid-fire laboratory techniques, overplayed scientific deduction, and dramatic acting meant that every forensic case is solved in 45 minutes.

This was not a forensic identification operation carried out in dramatically darkened rooms with clever lighting effects. In the words of one of the ICMP's DNA technicians, when you are working with DNA identification, what you need in a laboratory are three things: light, light, and more light. The ICMP's operations were real-life, human *CSI*: sad, practical, often smelly and tear-stained, and always remorselessly human. They were on the front lines of forensic science. Every bone sample was a human story, every blood sample a scarlet drop that spelled grief, anguish, uncertainty, loss, and endless waiting. The samples represented not just the missing persons from whose bodies they had been taken, but also the families' heartbreak back at home, as they waited desperately to know what had happened.

The ICMP's facilities, by 2010, included the former funeral home in Lukavac, outside Tuzla. Here a Canadian forensic anthropologist and her team from the Lukavac Reassociation Centre emptied body bags and then pieced together the disarticulated skeletons of the victims of Srebrenica. Visitors to this facility and the mortuary at the Podrinje Identification Project often found it disturbing, but also found that the sheer reality explained the nature of what the ICMP did better than any introductory words. The pungent smell of decay and death, the body bags, and the hundreds of bodies proved too much for some. At the Tuzla mortuary, a hard-bitten television cameraman who'd seen the worst of war just went white, started sweating, and went outside. A journalist walked into the mortuary, took one look, and fainted, unconscious before she nearly hit the floor. (Fortunately, an ICMP staffer caught her.) An A-list international film actor, in Bosnia to research a role, almost vomited when a body bag's contents were shown to him. A right-wing European politician who had voiced doubts before arriving in Tuzla as to whether the hideous tale of Srebrenica was exactly correct was converted at the Lukavac funeral parlor. "So it really *did* happen," he was heard to exclaim after watching staff empty body bags.

One of many things that makes organizations like the ICMP stand out is that they offer the possibility for the technical wonderment of science, the physical presence of human suffering, and the workings of a large international organization to coexist under one roof. Gray-faced relatives of the missing trudge broken-spirited into the reception area, their cried-out faces bearing testimony to how life has let them down. They give their blood samples and dutifully hand over their mobile phone numbers, then drift off, back into a life of huge absences. The ICMP staff, meanwhile, like many human beings who work in the presence of, and on the front lines of, mass, violent death, can be wonderful ambassadors for the human spirit. Like many individuals that deal on a daily basis with the violent results of war and ethnic conflict, working in the world of practical forensic science and missing persons, they show that for every gram of human misery there is an equivalent measure of human kindness and levity of the human spirit.

By 2010, the International Commission on Missing Persons had spread its forensic wings globally. First, what it had done in Bosnia had led the Serbian authorities to ask for its assistance in overseeing forensic exhumations of Kosovo Albanians. Then it had branched out into Disaster Victim Identification with the Asian tsunami and Hurricane Katrina. Simultaneously, the request for assistance came from Chile, while ICMP was drafting a report that would help the Colombian government in formulating laws to deal with persons missing from its internecine civil conflict. Then came the Philippines, then Norway, then the enormous Iraq mission, with, along the way, requests for help from countries such as South Africa, Cyprus, and Kuwait. When the former British foreign secretary said that the ICMP's organization and facilities had become a global center of excellence, he was not being overly effusive.

Forensic officials from Moscow dealing with counterterrorism in Chechnya and Moscow would pass through the ICMP's doors, and the next day there'd be a delegation of family associations from El Salvador visiting the Sarajevo laboratory in the morning and being briefed by Kathryne Bomberger in the afternoon. On their way out of the head-quarters they might cross paths with a group of American exchange students in international relations interning in Europe for the holidays. Or there would be the bulletproof Audis gliding to a stop outside the main entrance and the bodyguards with their functional suits and ubiq-uitous Oakley sunglasses—even in winter—which meant a minister from somebody's government or a senior ambassador. And all the while, threading through the constant visitors, came the Bosnian families who had come to give blood samples, who sat nervously in reception, tissues scrunched in palms, eyes red from recent tears, waiting to go through and leave their pinpricks of scarlet hope.

Chapter Eleven

RATKO MLADIĆ'S LAST REQUEST

W hich one of you is the American?" asked Ratko Mladić of the fourteen Serbian policemen who came to his cousin's house to arrest him at 5:00 am on May 26, 2011. After sixteen years on the run, Mladić must have thought constantly that when the end came, it would involve American Special Forces, a shootout, helicopters, and search-lights. But the end, when it did come, was rather more prosaic.

Mladić's cousin Branko owns a house at number 2 Vuk Karadžić Street in the small Serbian town of Lazarevo, which sits some 50 miles northeast of Belgrade on the agricultural plains of Vojvodina province. The whitewashed, one-story building, set in a compound behind a red iron gate, has some plum, apple, and pear trees in the garden and to all extents and purposes looks like any number of other rural houses across the Balkans. Nenad Popovic, Branko's next-door neighbor, reported that when he went outside to water his peppers before the sun came up on the morning of May 26, he could see fourteen policemen, four of them in uniform, ten of them in plainclothes.[1] They seemed concerned and were milling around and peering in through the windows of the guest house in the garden.

They knocked on the wooden door of the small house, and when there was no answer, they entered it. Popovic returned to his peppers.

Inside the guesthouse, the policemen, who were from the Belgrade Interior Ministry's police, encountered an elderly looking man in a tracksuit walking toward them. When they asked him his name, he simply replied that he was the man they had been looking for. They pinned him to the ground and later discovered two guns in the house, a Yugoslav 7.65 mm Zastava and an American Beretta. The police officers took him outside and sat him on the front step as they searched the house. Across the town of Lazarevo, police officers were also searching three other houses, all of them belonging to distant relatives of Ratko Mladić. Mladić boasted to the policemen that he could have killed ten of them with his handguns—he claimed he didn't because they were just young and doing their job. These claims instantly sounded hollow: when the police officers dressed Mladić, they discovered that one of his arms was numb and powerless, the result of a stroke he had suffered two years earlier. He was taken back outside, put into one of the vehicles, and driven to Belgrade.

The version above was the clearest record of events reported in the days and weeks surrounding the arrest. A second, highly plausible and well-sourced version of events is that a small group of policemen were following Mladić's family members who had gone to Lazarevo, thinking that they might lead them to the fugitive general. Julian Borger, the diplomatic editor of the *Guardian*, investigated the story in considerable depth, and his reporting about Mladić's time on the run is probably the most authoritative to date. He says that one or a few policemen went to Lazarevo that day, found Mladić hiding in the house, and the subsequent arrest with other police officers proceeded from there. He also claims that President Tadić vowed it was something that happened spontaneously, and the Serbian authorities had not known where Mladić was in advance.[2]

Either way, that morning Mladić appeared before the Belgrade High Court to determine if he was fit to travel to The Hague: the ruling judge suspended the hearings, as he said that because of his health there was no way that Mladić could even communicate properly. But Mladić managed to talk to one of the war crimes prosecutors, and so the court ruled that he was fit to travel to Holland on May 27. In the interim he was taken to Belgrade's central prison, where his old friend Zoran Stankovic, the former director of Belgrade's military hospital, visited him. Stankovic was now health minister for the country. He talked to Mladić and arranged to try and negotiate with the court to see if Mladić could make one last trip into central Belgrade before he was extradited to The Hague. The former general wanted to go to the Topcider cemetery and visit his daughter's grave. He was allowed to and was taken to the cemetery in a white armored vehicle, escorted by a black Land Rover and two minibuses filled with special police. The prosecutor said they'd allowed Mladić to visit the grave because it was a private matter. Because it represented a security risk, no announcement was made about it in advance. Mladić left a bouquet of white flowers with a single red rose in the middle and lit a candle for his daughter. The whole operation, from courthouse cell to the cemetery and back again, took 22 minutes.

By late that morning, Serbian president Boris Tadić gave a press conference where they announced the news of Mladić's capture. From Belgrade outward, word quickly spread. Ministers, officials in The Hague Tribunal, reporters, and the population of the region were used to false alarms and rumors about Mladić. In 2006 he reportedly had already been in the custody of British Special Forces and Romanian police in a small village on Serbia's border before The Hague prosecutor Carla del Ponte had issued a statement denying the allegations. Tadić said simply that Mladić had been arrested and added few details of what had happened. He and other Serbian government officials immediately started to stress that Serbia's accession process to the European Union, which had been frozen by Mladić's long period at liberty, could now be unblocked. The Serbian interior minister was due to meet officials from the European

Union in Belgrade on May 31, officials who oversaw the 27–nation bloc's membership accession criteria. In short, Tadić was beginning to do all the things a country needed to do, ticking all the boxes he needed to tick, to join the EU. Serbia's senior official responsible for EU enlargement remarked shortly afterward that Mladić's arrest was not going to be a panacea for all the country's problems, or, as she said, a joker that would trump all the other cards that Serbia had stacked against it.[3]

In The Hague, Nerma Jelačić, who had fled Visegrad in 1992, was now spokesperson and head of communications services for the ICTY. She had heard about the news of the arrest from one of her colleagues. Realizing that Ratko Mladić, who was then the most wanted man in the world following the death of Osama bin Laden, would be arriving shortly at the United Nations' detention facility at Scheveningen outside the capital, she started to prepare requisite statements to give to the hundreds of journalists whom she knew would be beating a path to her door.

The Hague's immediate priority was to get Mladić to the Dutch court safe and sound, in one piece. Mladić's lawyer filed an appeal to resist extradition on the grounds of ill health, but the extradition appeal was turned down, and Mladić was driven to Belgrade's airport for a flight to Rotterdam on a Serbian government jet on May 31.

The jet landed at the Dutch airport and taxied into a hangar, outside of which a helicopter landed. Mladić, shielded by police vehicles, was escorted into the helicopter and flown to the detention center for administrative and health checks before appearing in court to enter his initial pleas. Across the Balkans and Europe and in the United States, reactions to his arrest poured in, and from them it was possible to judge how far the much-vaunted reconciliatory aims of the international community had come since the end of the Bosnian war in 1995.

It was also interesting to see the reactions of the relatives of Mladić's victims, given the stunning amount of forensic and human rights assistance they'd received. Was this the last piece of the forensic science puzzle falling into place? Had the cycles of justice, reconciliation, forensics, and human rights now come full circle? Who was pleased by the news? Who was furious? Who cared? Who didn't? The arrest seemed to focus all of the worries and concerns and priorities, the achievements and grievances and self-promotion, of all of the countries, communities, politicians, interest groups, families, and individuals whose lives had been, since the beginning of the Bosnian war, touched by Ratko Mladić.

One of the people who had had an enormous amount to do with Mladić for over a decade was Andrew Cayley, the British Queen's Counsel,[4] who had worked as a senior prosecutor on the Mladić case at the ICTY. He had also worked afterward at the International Criminal Court in The Hague and at the Special Court for Sierra Leone. By 2009, he was the international co-prosecutor at the Phnom Penh war crimes tribunal,[5] set up to try the most senior former Khmer Rouge commanders responsible for the Cambodian genocide. The greatest responsibility the Yugoslav tribunal now had, he said in 2012, was to try Mladić fairly. This was vital.

At the opening of the Nuremberg trials on November 11, 1945, the chief prosecutor, Robert H. Jackson, said, "That four great nations, flushed with victory and stung with injury stay the hand of vengeance and voluntarily submit their captive enemies to the judgment of the law is one of the most significant tributes that Power has ever paid to Reason."[6] This is as true today as it was then, said Cayley, adding that whatever is felt about his crimes, the very fact that Mladić was subjected to the sober judgment of the law reminds and reassures that decency does, and indeed must, govern and rule over the affairs of humanity.

Cayley added that he'd spent ten years prosecuting at the International Criminal Tribunal for the former Yugoslavia in The Hague, and Mladić, as chief of staff of the Bosnian Serb Army, was implicated in the worst of the arrogance, brutality, and annihilation of the Bosnian war, Sarajevo, Srebrenica, and Prijedor. "At Srebrenica, where thousands of men and boys were murdered, he was 'the angel of death,' a swaggering, threatening evil figure who bullied and terrified weak and helpless people," says Cayley. "He was still a hero in Serbia, though, and would never have been accused there. He could only face justice before the international courts. Why was the case important?"

It was very simple. "Because the majority of people who suffered and died in Bosnia are like us," says Cayley. "They were not involved in the controversies of the time. They wanted to be safe, they loved their children, and they hated war. It is for these ordinary people that this trial is so very important. The Office of the Prosecutor [OTP] painstakingly constructed the case against Mladić: it exhumed thousands of bodies from mass graves—victims of Srebrenica—and they seized military documents from Bosnian Serb military units. It took so long for Mladić to be arrested because he was seen as a Serbian hero. For years he was protected by military and political figures in Belgrade. This is a fact and should never be forgotten."[7]

Almost immediately after the news of the arrest broke, 10,000 demonstrators took to the streets of Banja Luka. Bojo Gusic, a Bosnian Serb war veteran, said simply that he loved his general and loved freedom, and so he had come out on the streets to support a man he considered a hero. Meanwhile, in Sarajevo and across Bosnia, the families of Mladić's victims gave their reactions to his arrest. The most carefully prepared summary of these reactions was presented in a condensed book form by the offices of the Balkans Investigative Reporting Network. This group had worked assiduously to do its part in bringing war criminals to justice, properly documenting and recording the process of national and international trials. One facet of this report was a collection of quotes and reactions to Mladić's arrest that gave evidence of the different Bosnian mindsets at the time.[8] "We urge The Hague Tribunal that the trial of Ratko Mladić be fair, quick and efficient, so that all of the victims of the war may welcome the verdict," said the president of the Parents of Children Killed in Besieged Sarajevo, Fikret Grabovica.

One of Sarajevo's leading dailies, *Dnevni Avaz*, printed an editorial that summed up the Bosnian Muslim view of Ratko Mladić: "The criminal loves attention, and wants to give an impression about who's the boss. He knows the mentality of the people very well, and plays on the fact that we are merciful, even towards felons. He does not want to give the impression of a wretch. He thinks he did everything according to the law: he is someone who wants to kill."[9] Fahrudin Radončić, the president of the Alliance for a Better Future for Bosnia and Herzegovina political party in Sarajevo, said that "Srebrenica's executioner" was facing justice too late, and that his arrest had only come as a consequence of pressure from the European Union, and because Serbia wanted to join it and access its development funding.[10] One survivor of Srebrenica, with reconciliation very much not on his mind, said, "[Mladić] is a zero of a man. God punished him, but still did not punish him enough. His punishment would be to never die. I want that curse to reach him, in Bosnian, Serbian and Croatian, because during three years of the Srebrenica siege we were dying in the town from his shells."[11]

On the other side of the ethnic coin, Serbs across Bosnia predominantly bemoaned the arrest and his subsequent transfer to The Hague. The president of the Republika Srpska, Nebojša Radmanović, said that the arrest was an emotional experience for Serbs.

Nezavisne Novine, one of the two main newspapers in the Bosnian Serb capital, Banja Luka, stood up for Mladić in a remarkable editorial on May 29: quoting the inhabitants of Bozanovic, Mladić's home village near Kalinovik in Bosnia, the paper noted that the general was "a nice man, naturally intelligent, the best scholar and attendant of the military academy, a man who would not hurt a fly, a Serbian hero, an honorable soldier, a protector of Muslims." The newspaper went on to quote a noted Serbian poet and self-declared "intellectual," Rajko Petrov Nogo, who said that the arrest of Mladić marked what he called "the punch-line of decades of Serbian humiliation, it is the humiliation of a whole nation."[12]

Victims, politicians, and commentators on all sides were playing to their physical and psychosocial electorate. Perhaps one of the better quotes came from the Serbian daily *Vreme*. The paper questioned why Mladić had continued to remain so important to so many: the old guard and the new guard, those who were chasing him and those who were protecting him. The paper ascribed this obsession with Mladić to the national subconscious urge to preserve the idea of the former Yugoslavia: "The bankrupt project of Milošević and his fascist helper."[13]

Then the dust settled, and Mladić was safely in detention. The head-lines in Serbia had moved on from the last demands that Mladić made from his prison cell before being sent to The Hague—fresh strawberries and a selection of Russian literature, including the complete works of Tolstoy. The most obvious question remained to be answered properly. Why had Mladić—who, according to neighbors, Serbian intelligence, the ICTY, and others, had been living in Lazarevo for at least three years—not been arrested before? Was the answer that the Serbian state didn't arrest him out of lack of necessity? Or it couldn't, because it had no idea where he was? Or wouldn't, because it was being blocked by external or internal interests?

Kurt Bassuener, the American political analyst based in Sarajevo, said that it was a combination of factors. First, the chief prosecutor of the ICTY, Serge Brammertz, believed that Serbia did not want to coop-erate with The Hague and only did so because Tadić's government saw this cooperation as vital for inclusion in the European Union. President Boris Tadić had prioritized EU membership, which he thought was the country's ticket out of its recent past. Second, the Dutch government had power of veto over Serbia's accession and was prepared to base its judgment on Brammertz's opinion. Third, Irish members of Parliament had held hearings on Mladić's status and had asked the Serbian foreign minister Vuk Jeremić to testify in Dublin in January 2011.

The fact that two EU members were looking into applying conditionality to ratify Serbia's Stability and Association Agreement (part of the EU accession process), and presumably EU candidacy after that, on a war crimes compliance basis spooked Tadić. It was a simple cost-benefit analysis. Bassuener believes that until that point, Tadić thought he could get what he wanted for free. When confronted by an immovable object and a potentially increasing price tag in advance of contentious elections, he decided it was time to "pony up and find Mladić."[14]

The arrest was a matter of timing. Serbia was getting no conceivable benefit from Mladić's continued presence on Serbian territory—in fact, his presence was hurting them. The International Monetary Fund had just announced they were delaying a loan tranche, and the EU said that further pre-accession grants were suspended until the former Bosnian general was transferred to Holland. Other factors were also involved. Tadić's camp knew that the arrest could be a major snub to the nationalist old guard of Vojislav Koštunica and the Serbian Radical Party, whom the president reportedly had issues with. He also knew that Mladić was likely to give testimony that would seriously incriminate both of these parties. So the word went out to the intelligence agents of the domestic intelligence service, Bezbednosno Informativna Agencija, the policemen of the Interior Ministry, and by connection every federal officer on the beat across Serbia that Mladić was to be detained on sight.

The decision in 2006 by The Hague prosecutor, Carla del Ponte, to urge Serbia's War Crimes Court to arrest the twelve to fifteen individuals who were then sheltering Mladić in New Belgrade pushed him to seek shelter with his extended family and probably lengthened the period that Mladić was able to spend on the run. After the arrest of this network, he was not extensively in touch with what the British general

David Leakey had called "any known associates." Therefore, the easiest thing for him to do was hide with relatives in the riverside suburb of Mala Moštanica and afterward pay for one last trip to Lazarevo before his remaining protectors—who were no longer interested in the prospect of a fifteen-year jail sentence for looking after a past-his-sell-by-date national hero—simply disappeared.

In The Hague, at Last

The main entrance of the former insurance building that houses the International Criminal Tribunal for the former Yugoslavia sits behind the wide boulevard of Churchillplein in the Dutch capital. On the main door there is a large, plastic-laminated sign posted prominently. Illustrated on it in black and red are all of the different kinds of weapons that are forbidden inside the building. It is an exhaustive pictorial list of 29 items: there are sub-machine guns, knuckle-dusters, Tasers, hand grenades, rapiers, cutlasses, throwing stars, rifles, silenced pistols, and eight different kinds of knives.

However, after passing through the elaborate security procedure, smartly dressed United Nations security guards in ironed blue shirts and dark blue trousers with holstered 9 mm automatics on their belts tell incoming visitors that the most routine security threat is from visiting parties of schoolchildren dropping their ice creams. Another staff member says that in five years of working at the ICTY, the most conspicuous and vocal threat to security has been from outraged and dissatisfied Mothers of Srebrenica and Žepa protesting at the defendants through the bulletproof glass that separates the public gallery from each of the three separate courtrooms.

In the main atrium with its shining marble floor, past the security guards, there are huge posters. "Bringing Justice to Victims, Holding Leaders Accountable, Individualizing Guilt, Giving Victims a Voice, Establishing the Facts, Strengthening the Rule of Law, Developing

International Law" lists one, which are the seven priorities of the ICTY. "161 Individuals Indicted, 0 Fugitives, Over 7,000 Trial Days, More than 4,000 witnesses" says another poster. At the bottom of it is the message: "Thanks to the ICTY the question is no longer whether leaders should be held accountable but rather when they will be called to account."

On Wednesday, May 16, 2012, just under seventeen years since Srebrenica, Ratko Mladić walked into court in an off-blue suit and checkered silk tie: the electric blinds that separate the glass walls of the public gallery from the courtroom purred and clicked upward—the hearings were not "in camera," or in private, away from the public, and there was Mladić for the world to see. The packed public gallery was full of Mothers of Srebrenica and Žepa. As the defendant looked over at them, one of them reportedly extended her middle finger at him. He smirked and drew a finger across his throat in an unmistakable gesture. Repentance was not on Mladić's agenda. He gave a confident and cheery thumbs-up as the judges, headed by Alphonse Orie, walked in. He called the accusations "monstrous," and on his behalf the court entered a not guilty plea. The first day the court heard, from the prosecution headed by Dermot Groome, that former general Ratko Mladić had intended to "ethnically cleanse" Bosnia. The first part of the hearing was given over to the prosecution, who showed a video recording filmed in 1993 in which Mladić and a Canadian cameraman of Serbian origin are talking.[15]

"Every time I go by Sarajevo, I kill someone in passing," says Mladić on the recording. "I kick the hell out of the *Balija* [Turks—a derogatory term for Bosnian Muslims]. Who cares what happens to them?" The prosecution then said that they intended to prove Mladić's involvement in the crimes he was charged with. "Four days ago marked two decades since Ratko Mladić became the commander of the main staff of the army of Republika Srpska—the VRS," Groome said. "On that day, Mladić began his full participation in a criminal endeavor that was already in progress. On that day, he assumed the mantle of realizing through military might the criminal goals of ethnically cleansing much of Bosnia. On that day, he commenced his direct involvement in serious international crimes. By the time he and his troops had murdered thousands in Srebrenica they were well-rehearsed in the craft of murder."[16]

The trial was to ricochet between suspension and session from its opening onward. On May 17 the trial was suspended indefinitely after the prosecution admitted that they had not disclosed the full list of their witnesses and witness testimony to the court. By January 2013 Mladić was facing former British general Sir Rupert Smith in court. Mladić accused him of having come to Bosnia on a personal mission to fight Serbs and claimed that the NATO airstrikes launched under Operation Deliberate Force were an attempt by Smith to humiliate Mladić. The claim was solipsistic, to say the least. Mladić's defense claimed that as NATO's ordnance had been directed toward an area where Mladić's predecessors were buried, it was an attempt by Smith to embarrass Mladić by demonstrating that he was not capable of protecting the burial areas of his ancestors, a traditional family obligation. Smith's dry and curt reply was that he was not remotely bothered whether the defendant was humiliated or not; he was only interested in preventing any further attacks on "safe havens," areas like Srebrenica.[17]

The prosecution had a very strong case against Mladić. First, the ICTY had found guilty and sentenced many of Mladić's subordinates who had been part of the command-and-control structure during the Bosnian Serb Army operations around Srebrenica. They knew a great deal about exactly what they could prove, and what they couldn't. They had learned the pitfalls of overzealous prosecution from previous trials. In one trial judgment, for instance, they had erred on the side of judicial caution when they said that they could not prove beyond a reasonable measure of doubt that one particular unit, or any members thereof, of the Bosnian Serb Army had been involved in executions around Srebrenica.[18]

Second, precedent had been set. In the cases of Radislav Krstić and others, the chain of command of the Bosnian Serb Army structure had been established. The prosecution could cite prior convictions as legally established fact. Third, the trial of Ratko Mladić for his alleged crimes was among the last taking place in The Hague, and the prosecution knew exactly which witnesses from previous cases could bring evidence that would add weight to their case. And they'd had a decade in which to discover and unearth new evidence. What might have been unknown in 2005, or existed simply as hearsay, could potentially be proven by 2012 and 2013. Fourth, the forensic evidence against Mladić in 2013 was much stronger than it would have been in 2001 or 2005. Simply put, more mass graves had been exhumed and more DNA matches made of the victims of Srebrenica. The forensic evidence that had been provided in court in the trials against Zdravko Tolimir and others had been tried and tested for its workability as evidence. The numbers stood up to scrutiny, as it were.

The International Commission on Missing Persons could bring DNA match reports to be used in court by both prosecution and defense, which provided material evidence based upon the work of the ICMP laboratory system. The ICMP's material evidence had been used in the *Popovic et al.* trial, which included five main Srebrenica defendants that came to judgment in 2010.

In its summary of the verdict in the case of *Popovic et al.*, the Trial Chamber mentioned the figure of 5,336 "identified individuals." The key word here was "identified": this number referred only to those victims of killings around Srebrenica that the ICMP had been able to identify, using DNA matches, at the time when they were asked to provide material, written, or expert evidence either to the prosecution or defense in The Hague. By the time Ratko Mladić arrived in court in Holland this number had risen substantially. By early February 2013, the ICMP were reporting that the number of DNA matches made of Srebrenica victims was almost

6,850, some 88 percent of the alleged total of around 8,100 persons estimated missing. The ICMP had provided evidence in previous trials at the ICTY and, at the time of writing, was preparing evidence to be submitted to the ICTY following requests by both prosecution and defense in the trial of Radovan Karadžić. It remained to be seen if the counsel defending or prosecuting Ratko Mladić would make such a submission request for evidence, but the ICMP was prepared to provide it if they did.

In *Popovic et al.*, the Trial Chamber's judgment also included the following findings:

> In the Prosecution's submission, the minimum number of persons that went missing or died following the fall of Srebrenica can be estimated to be 7,826....The Trial Chamber is satisfied beyond reasonable doubt that at least 5,336 identified individuals were killed in the executions following the fall of Srebrenica. The Trial Chamber also notes that the evidence before it is not all encompassing. Graves continue to be discovered and exhumed to this day, and the number of identified individuals will rise. The Trial Chamber therefore considers that the number could well be as high as 7,826.[19]

In May 2010 the expert witness Dusan Janc, previously an OTP investigator, testified at the ICTY in the trial of Zdravko Tolimir using the most recently updated version of the report compiled by his former office. According to the results of the investigation published in the latest OTP report, valid through the end of April 2010, "the number of identified Srebrenica victims has reached 6,557. There are still about 1,300 names on the list of the International Commission for Missing Persons whose remains have neither been recovered nor identified."[20]

The work done by the ICMP to exhume and identify human remains had, thus far, six main tangible results. First, they had given to women like Kada Hotic the physical bodies of their relatives to bury, providing vital closure and allowing them to have final proof that their male relatives had not, as Kathryne Bomberger had said, been deleted because of who they were. (By the time Mladić came to trial, Hotic's son Samir had been found and identified. In 2013, her brother Mustafa's head was found, identified, and buried.) Second, the work had added substantially to regional reconciliation efforts. Third, by identifying almost all of the pieces of the forensic science jigsaw puzzle, the organization had provided a clear and thorough documentation of history. Fourth, as was being proved each day in courtrooms one, two, and three at The Hague, the ICMP was enabling successful prosecutions of the allegedly guilty parties, and thus providing justice. Fifth, it had seen the establishment of a verifiable and workable forensic and human rights system that could be deployed in other countries, like Iraq. And lastly, it was a scientific success story, albeit one derived from enormous human sadness and loss, that showed Bosnia and the capacity of its people at their best.

In November 2006 the ICMP and the ICTY's former chief prosecutor, Carla del Ponte, exchanged letters on assistance, in which the OTP acknowledged the ICMP's important functions and the safeguards it required. They pledged to work together to secure the necessary funding for the ICMP's assistance to criminal justice. The ICMP then met in January 2008 with the new prosecutor, Serge Brammertz, who expressed his gratitude to them for their assistance and requested its continuation, which he regarded as essential to the work of the ICTY and the OTP.[21]

The activities that the ICMP were carrying out in the field of justice included providing summary updates on DNA and exhumation work; providing analytical updates relative to specific events (e.g., the fall of Srebrenica); writing individual case reports on specific DNA identifications; collecting waivers from family members to allow the use of their genetic information in trial; preparing reports on excavations of mass grave sites, including linking these graves; and preparing and giving expert witness statements and testimony. The waivers from the family members were vital: the relatives of the victims had to give their consent before the DNA match reports could be used in court. Obtaining these waivers and this consent could take months, but the extremely high level of education about legal and human rights that family members of missing persons received via their associations and via the ICMP now proved their worth.

The ICMP had, by early 2013, supported the ICTY with testimony, statements, and depositions *inter alia* in a variety of high-profile cases involving the deaths of thousands of people, regarding not just Srebrenica but war crimes committed across the rest of the former Yugoslavia, including some allegedly carried out by Kosovo Albanians, Macedonians, and Croatians. Their expertise had been brought to bear in domestic war crimes trials in Bosnia and Herzegovina. At the time of writing, the ICMP's assistance is being sought, by both the prosecution and the accused, in the case of *Prosecutor vs. Radovan Karadžić*.[22] The ICMP documentation reads as such:

> Following lengthy discussions occasioned by Mr. Karadžić demanding full access to ICMP databases and systems, the Chamber is currently ruling on a compromise proposal to request from ICMP a random selection of 300 cases considered by the prosecution as related to the fall of Srebrenica. Providing 300 DNA case files and related testimony will be the single most sizeable measure of assistance that ICMP extends to ICTY. It will incur seeking over 1,600 permissions from surviving relatives to use their genetic information in trial, as well as compiling over 9,000 pages of evidence from various ICMP departments. ICMP hopes to complete the case-files within six months as of notification by either the Chamber or OTP. The subsequent duration and frequency of testimony and cross-examination cannot be ascertained at this time.
>
> ICMP expects that evidence introduced in the case of *Prosecutor vs. Radovan Karadžić* will also be admitted in the trial of Ratko Mladić. In

that event, ICMP's assistance may be limited to providing testimony. While assistance in other trials has not been requested to date, ICMP cannot rule out that it will be receiving such requests, in particular in the context of domestic war crimes trials. ICMP's assistance to the ICTY contributes to that court's completion strategy, and would hence end in 2014 when the court is scheduled to close. As concerns domestic prosecutions, it should be expected that demand for ICMP evidence and testimony will continue beyond 2014. That situation would change only if the current domestic practice that disallows the use of evidence from ICTY trials in domestic trials was discontinued. The ICMP's exit strategy, as far as assistance to justice is concerned, is hence linked to procedural aspects of the criminal code of Bosnia and Herzegovina.[23]

The appearance of the ICMP's forensic evidence in court in The Hague was not just going to be the last part of the forensic science puzzle; it was going to be the convincing proof that methodically and properly deployed scientific technique could judicially triumph. Scientific truth, and by extension justice, could triumph over hearsay, rumor, conspiracy theory, the fallibilities of human evidence—memory, visual recollection—lying, and planned deceit. In the cases mentioned above, it had been the moment when modern forensic techniques coupled with carefully honed judicial deployment went toe to toe with revisionist history and distorted knowledge and won the day. What the ICMP had achieved, and was achieving, in terms of justice and reconciliation can be summed up by two of those who best saw its results and effects. The Hague Tribunal's prosecutor Serge Brammertz said at the end of 2012[24] that the fact that the ICTY indicted 161 mostly high-level politicians and military personnel, and that no indictee remained at large, was an exceptional achievement. No other international tribunal could present such a record, and many thought this was impossible when the tribunal was created. The successful arrests of high-level accused were of huge significance to the victims. Redress for their suffering was long over-due, Brammertz said, noting "prosecutions can have a positive impact on reconciliation in the region."

The tribunal has generated a huge corpus of jurisprudence, which has contributed extensively to the development of international criminal law, and the ICTY has set standards and norms that serve as examples for other international and national courts in a field of the law that had seen little adjudication since Nuremberg. Brammertz also considered the transition toward local prosecutions critical, saying that the ICTY's success depended on this, and that it had strongly supported all initiatives to strengthen local prosecutions and the rule of law more generally. "But that work is not over," he said. "For instance, in Bosnia and Herzegovina more than 800 war crimes cases are yet to be prosecuted, and a lot of work remains to be done to complete these remaining cases. It is like a sword of Damocles hanging above Bosnia. The future stability of Bosnia depends upon ensuring that the rule of law is strengthened and perpetrators of crimes are brought to justice."[25]

Standing in front of the ICTY's headquarters, watching large Atlantic gulls that have winged in from the North Sea pull hanks of tufty grass with their sharp bills out of The Hague Tribunal's lawn, Nerma Jelačić drew on a Marlboro Light. Well versed, to say the least, in all aspects of Balkan war crimes, she says that the ICMP's work has been crucial for the establishment of the truth about the war in Bosnia, and not only over Srebrenica. The enormous historical significance of such achievements is not always recognized and celebrated, particularly at the time. After such a tragedy befell Bosnia and Herzegovina, the survivors were blessed to have had a forensic revolution. Until the ICMP existed she had not been aware of any other country that had such a high rate of identifications of missing persons.

But, she reflected, this is something that would probably only be fully appreciated by wider society from a historical distance. "Until then,

I am sure the biggest and the most important appreciation of ICMP's work comes from those most affected by it—the bereaved who were, thanks to the ICMP, able to identify their loved ones and lay them to rest," she says. "Of course, the importance of these identifications and statistics held by ICMP for successful prosecution of war crimes cannot be undermined, nor forgotten, either. Numerous are the cases before the tribunal where ICMP expert testimony and material evidence formed the backbone to the facts established in the judgments. In that sense, it is a perfect example of how criminal prosecutions and other methods of transitional justice work together to build the road to bridge legacies of wars."[26]

Chapter Twelve

FROM SREBRENICA TO KURDISTAN, BRAZZAVILLE, AND LIBYA

On the second day of winter snowfall of 2012, which came in the first week of December that year, British, American, and Bosnian forensic experts from the Sarajevo office of the International Commission on Missing Persons were preparing to deploy to the West African city of Brazzaville, the capital of the Republic of Congo. A week before, an Ilyushin aircraft, on a routine cargo run from the Congolese port city of Pointe Noire, had crashed during a thunderstorm into a heavily populated shantytown around the Brazzaville airport. Thirty people, including six Armenian crew members, were reportedly killed instantly. In the French city of Lyons, Interpol received a request from the Congolese government to immediately send a team to assist with Disaster Victim Identification. The international police organization wasted no time: they contacted the ICMP, now the world's acknowledged leader in the grisly but vital field of Disaster Victim Identification.

Ian Hanson, who had exhumed mass graves and burial sites in Bosnia, the Democratic Republic of the Congo, Guatemala, Iraq, and the Egyptian pyramids, was in the office when the call came through, preparing to travel to Libya. The ICMP was establishing an advisory and training mission in that country that would help them find and identify the thousands of persons who went missing during the regime of Colonel

Muammar al-Gaddafi, and in previous conflicts. Around him the office of the forensics department was hectic. Esma Aličehagjić, a permanently smiling, highly talented, and glamorous British-Bosnian forensic archaeologist, was off to Sarajevo hospital to get yellow fever shots for possible travel to the Congo; Matthew Vennemeyer, an American forensic expert and veteran of exhuming victims of Saddam Hussein from landmine-strewn desert graves in the Sunni Triangle, was preparing blood, bone, and human tissue sampling kits for the Brazzaville plane crash. Hanson was on the line to Erbil in Kurdistan, where Adam Boys was overseeing staff deployments, and was simultaneously e-mailing Sydney, asking for advice about the Congo from his mentor, the erudite Australian forensic archaeologist Richard Wright. At the Bosnian HQ of the ICMP, it was a busy day in the office. Real-life *CSI* was in action.

Three time zones to the east, North Carolinian David Hines, the ICMP's training coordinator in the areas controlled by the Regional Government of Kurdistan, was winding down his day in Erbil, Kurdistan's dusty capital. He'd been working as a death investigator for a medical examiner's office in the United States when he first got a job in Iraq to investigate mass graves. He and a small group of colleagues were now the front line in the largest ICMP mission since the Balkans.

Iraq was, in military terminology, a boots-on-ground mission. Hines had first worked with the forensic exhumation teams set up in the wake of the American occupation of and deployment into Iraq in 2003, tasked with dealing with war crimes committed under the rule of Saddam Hussein. The formal title of the unit was the Regime Crimes Liaison Office, Mass Graves Investigation Team, run by the US Army Corps of Engineers, which employed archaeologists. At that time the work of investigating mass graves in Iraq was done entirely by internationals. Hines worked the job from 2005 to 2007, when the forensic segment of the work was transferred to the Iraqis. Hines went back to America and in 2010 took a job with the ICMP's training mission in Iraq.

Erbil seemed a strange place to be based, and it was a long way from the early days of the ICMP in Sarajevo. With the mission in Kurdistan and Iraq, it almost seemed that the organization was moving at the speed of the news. It seemed that post-conflict countries were learning fast that there was now a specific organization that could help them deal with missing persons. And suddenly a number of countries all seemed to want help at the same time. The Americans funded the Iraq mission in the land of the Euphrates and Tigris rivers predominantly, with British and United Nations money thrown in as well. The broad aim was to train enough Iraqis in the basics of foreign investigation and forensic examination to be able to tackle the vast problem of persons missing in the country. Conservative estimates by Iraqi officials in the know put the lowest number of missing persons at 350,000. The maximum, including those missing from the regime of Saddam Hussein, his clampdowns on the Kurdish population and Marsh Arabs in the 1980s and the 1990s, two Gulf wars, the Iran–Iraq war, and the post-2003 insurgency was estimated to be as high as 1.5 million. And the methods and modus operandi that team members like Hines used to assist the Iraqis were those that the ICMP had learned so painstakingly in the Balkans. The task was enormous and included collecting blood, setting up a DNA identification center and laboratory facility, forming the families of the missing into associations that could fight for their social rights, and training experts in all aspects of the forensic science deemed necessary to deal with all of the mass graves scattered across the country.

The ICMP had started off with the rough estimate, given to them by the Iraqi forensic scientists who had been shuttling to and from the Sarajevo headquarters since late 2009, that there were around 250-plus mass graves in the country. Most of Iraq's mass graves contained victims of Saddam Hussein. Some people, in the aftermath of his overthrow in 2003, even began to dig up graves by themselves, a practice that was soon outlawed. Looking around himself in Erbil, the wise and reflective Hines was reminded of how much of a boomtown the capital of Kurdistan had become. People he met who grew up there would say things like, "I remember when this road was dirt." In 2003, the airport had consisted of a dirt runway with a windsock at the end; by 2010, a large terminal was being built. At every point of the compass, when he looked around in January 2013, David Hines could see a construction crane.

He was teaching familiar topics in Erbil: basic archaeology and basic anthropology, divided into two separate courses of learning. The archaeology students learned surveying, mapping, excavation, documentation, and recovery; the anthropology students studied anatomy, biological profiling (which involved determining age and sex), and pathology. The team had also created advanced training courses in photography, ground-penetrating radar, GIS mapping, commingled remains, report writing, mortuary management and logistics, and mass graves field management—in short, all of the skills that had served the ICMP so well in the Balkans. The training exercises included unearthing plastic skeletons buried in the garden of the hospital. The ICMP trainers tried to make the scenario as realistic as possible. Having a permanent team on the ground seemed to be enormously important. They'd trained staff and management and encouraged Iraqis to keep working on improving practices such as excavation skills, documentation, information tracking, and use of personnel.

The mass graves in Iraq were very different from the typical forensic experience. Before coming there, the largest number of people Hines had seen in a single grave was two, what he called "drug runners who'd run afoul of a guy in a motorcycle gang."

He continued, "If you have two bodies in a grave, you can do that in an afternoon, cops watching you, no problem. If you have 114 people in a grave, you're in there for a week. After you clean it off, you're going to be taking days to document everyone, figure out what order to pull them in. Sometimes in Iraq people didn't know they were going to be killed—often, with the Anfal graves of Kurds killed by Saddam's forces, what you're seeing is people who were told they were being relocated, so they brought a lot of their stuff with them. Luggage, belongings, lots of clothing. And they still have it when you excavate them. So you don't just see them, you see what was important to them. One six-year-old girl I excavated still had her airline bag in her hands. So you spend time with them, their stuff, and you get a snapshot of a community. It's a lot more intimate. You feel like you get to know them a little bit."[1]

The six-year-old girl with the airline bag still clutched in her hands could be a universal symbol of those executed for simply being who they were and who they'd been born. They were dug up only when their countries realized it was time to come to terms with and face the agonizing difficulties of dealing with their own pasts. To the southeast of David Hines, another country that needed help dealing with its past was receiving assistance from somebody who knew the business and the historical and psychological context. In 2012, shortly after Muammar al-Gaddafi's overthrow and subsequent death, the Libyans had asked the ICMP for help in dealing with some 8,000 missing persons.

In December 2012 the Libyan National Transitional Council decided it was time to tackle the thorny problem of those who had been forcibly disappeared and gone missing in the country over the previous 35 years. The council authorized the country's new Minister for Affairs of the Families of Martyrs and Missing Persons to handle this issue. Its minister, Mr. Naser Djibril Hamed, promptly approached the ICMP for assistance. He had committed to searching for persons in a nondiscriminatory fashion, regardless of whether the person missing was a "loyalist, rebel, or from another group."[2] He said there could be up to 10,000 persons missing in Libya, both from the recent conflict, as well as from the 1977 war with Egypt, the 1978 war with Uganda, the 1980–1987 wars with Chad, and the 1996 Abu Salim Prison massacre in Tripoli.

The bodies of the missing were scattered in mass graves across the country, and to come up with a strategy to find, exhume, and identify them, Hamed visited Sarajevo in spring 2012, professing himself very impressed with the ICMP's work in Bosnia, which, he said, had provided a very good model for them. The ICMP, Kathryne Bomberger said, had modernized and transformed the international community's response to the issue of missing persons. The organization would assist the Libyans by deploying the same operationally trifurcated approach that had reaped success in the Balkans: establishing forensic scientific expertise, cultivating a human rights–based approach to helping victims' living relatives, and creating legislation to help the fledgling Libyan authorities deal with missing persons. In time, Libyans intend to establish the Libya Identification Center, which will handle the location, recovery, and identification of the missing. Two non-governmental organizations, the Libyan Society for Missing Persons and the Free Generation Movement, were created to work on the *Mafqood*, or "missing," project; they recorded information on mass graves and used resources like Facebook to collect tallies of missing persons. In time, a DNA-assisted identification process will hopefully be created in Libya, drawing on the expertise of the ICMP's Sarajevo laboratory. By the end of the first full month of operations working on Libyan samples, the laboratory in Sarajevo had already generated nearly 100 DNA match reports.

The American government, mindful of the forensic and reconciliatory efficacy their donations to the ICMP programs in the Balkans and Iraq had bought, were providing 65 percent of the initial $1 million costs of the preliminary Libya project. Denmark was providing the remainder. By February 2013 the British government had pledged major funding for the project as well, providing the ICMP with a further $650,000 for use in Libya and the laboratory system back in Bosnia.

In the eighteen years since the ICMP's founding, doggedly loyal donor governments had stepped repeatedly up to the plate—the

Americans, the Dutch, the Swiss, the Swedes, the Norwegians, the British, the Germans, and the Spanish were among those governments who understood what the ICMP was doing, and why, and saw the need to provide them with the means to do it. The Iraq mission alone was, by early 2013, being funded by the Americans, the British, the Danish, the Germans, and the UN.

"Muammar Gaddafi and his regime," said Libya's minister Jibril Hamed, "stole a smile from the lips of many Libyan families through abduction and enforced disappearance of their children." He was talking in November 2012 in Tripoli, as he signed an agreement with the ICMP.

> Today we are striving to bring them their smile back and today I am delighted to sign this agreement with Ms. Kathryne Bomberger, the Director General of the International Commission on Missing Persons, ICMP, considering that ICMP is one of world's most important organizations engaged in the search and identification of missing persons. This has motivated us to seek cooperation with ICMP for the benefit of sons of the Libyan people who were disappeared by Gadhafi's regime during more than 42 years. The best proof of what this regime did are the cases of abduction and enforced disappearance during the 17th February Revolution. As we sign this agreement we ask the God Almighty to return hope to the families of the missing and we ask Him that we are drawing a path of hope for a better life.[3]

From Libya to Bosnia

Meanwhile, in Sarajevo, Adam Boys is still the chief operating officer and head of finance and administration, and to date has spent thirteen years with the ICMP; it has been nineteen years since he first arrived in Bosnia.

Good news is rare in Bosnia and Herzegovina. The country is still divided eighteen years after the war. It has a weak central government. Nevertheless, Boys is optimistic.

"ICMP's success could be said to be one of the most successful international interventions in post-conflict former Yugoslavia," he says. "Bosnia, and Bosnians especially, should be very proud of what has been achieved: other parts of the world are learning from the revolutionary approach that ICMP has developed."[4]

Meanwhile the ICMP had dispatched Muhamed Duraković, a new Bosnian staff member, to Tripoli as the head of the Libya Office. Duraković not only knew the forensic terrain, but he had intimate insight into the psychological turf and the difficulties of justice and reconciliation as well. After all, he grew up in Srebrenica. On July 11, 1995, he and his father had walked out of their garden, crossed the warm, summer fields of waving grass toward the edge of the forests, and started to run.

Since that fateful day, time has not stood still for him. After reaching safety, he'd worked for a Swedish aid agency in Tuzla, moved back to Sarajevo, studied in Philadelphia, and then returned to Bosnia, working initially for the international EU police mission and then for a government ministry. Part of his life vanished in Srebrenica, he says. There were men he wanted to invite to his wedding, to celebrate holidays with, and, when he was old, to go for walks in the hills with. But, as he says, "now they were almost all gone."

Bosnia and Herzegovina, as many countries before, he says, has been subjected to horrific crimes. Often, these crimes go unrecorded, allowing those who perpetrated them not only to go unpunished but also to deny historical facts. Through DNA profiling, it is possible to provide irrefutable evidence in the courts, making a big step toward justice and reconciliation. The work of the ICMP in Bosnia will be appreciated even more in the years to come, when the facts about the Bosnian war will be written with historical distance. Only then, he says, will the work of the International Commission on Missing Persons be appreciated to the fullest.

The ICMP comes with experience like no other organization. This will assist with the acceleration in the search for the missing in Libya. Duraković says he can connect with the Libyans on many different levels.

"I hope," he wrote, late one night from the heat of Tripoli, as the first days of the anniversary of the 2012 revolution approached, "to be able to utilize my experience in institution building, as well as in civil society development, to assist Libyans in the best way possible in closing this painful chapter in their recent history, and to give *our* contribution to the process of reconciliation and building of a better future for all Libyans."

Notes

Chapter One: How Does a Country Recover after a Genocide?

1   *Klen* are a coarse fish from the carp family, *Cyprinidae*, halfway between a chub and a barbel.

2   The author attended the conference as a guest.

3   Srebrenica was classified as an incidence of genocide in the judicial judgments, in particular, and the rulings and indictments of the International Criminal Tribunal for the former Yugoslavia, or ICTY, established and mandated by the United Nations in 1993 to deal with war crimes committed during the wars that accompanied the breakup of the former Yugoslavia.

4   The figure of 8,100 persons missing following the fall of Srebrenica was estimated following the reports of missing persons as presented and reported to the International Committee of the Red Cross (ICRC), the International Commission on Missing Persons (ICMP), the different missing persons commissions in each entity of Bosnia, and human rights groups

5   The exhumations of primary and secondary mass graves around Srebrenica and multiple rulings and judgments of the ICTY confirm this.

6   The use of aerial photographic imagery was to account for the location of many of the Srebrenica main execution and burial sites, along with witness testimony in The Hague, survivors' accounts, and examination of the terrain.

7   Reports from the Lukavac Reassociation Center, Tuzla, one of the facilities of the ICMP in Bosnia, 2009.

8   The term has existed regionally for over 150 years. The official United Nations definition of "ethnic cleansing" is "rendering an area ethnically homogeneous by using force or intimidation to remove from a given area persons of another ethnic or religious group" (UN Mission in Bosnia, International Criminal Tribunal for the former Yugoslavia).

9   The casualty figures come from the ICTY, the UN Commission of Experts, and the Sarajevo-based Research and Documentation Centre's "Book of the Dead."

10   Smith's astute analysis of modern warfare was summarized in his 2005 book *The Utility of Force: The Art of War in the Modern World* (London: Allen Lane, 2005).

11   This is the upper estimate of numbers used by the ICMP, based on numbers of persons reported missing to them, the ICRC, and the two missing persons commissions in Bosnia.

12   The final conflict in the breakup of Yugoslavia was the NATO bombing of Kosovo in 1999 designed to bring a halt to atrocities committed against Kosovo Albanians by President Milošević's forces.

13   The first conviction for genocide at The Hague Tribunal relating to crimes committed at Srebrenica was handed down to General Radislav Krstić on August 2, 2001: he was sentenced to 46 years in prison. This was later reduced on appeal to a lesser sentence of 35 years for aiding and abetting genocide.

14   The author reported extensively from Kosovo and Macedonia for British print media from 1999–2003.

Chapter Two: Separating the Men from the Women and Children in Srebrenica

1   In some areas, such as in Sarajevo, the ABiH contained Bosnian Serbs too.

2   Orić was convicted and sentenced to two years in prison by the ICTY in June 2006 for "failing to take steps to prevent the murder and cruel treatment of a number of Serb prisoners" on the basis of command responsibility. He was later acquitted of all charges on July 3, 2008, by the ICTY Appeals Chamber.

3   Interview with the author, Sarajevo, May 2010.

4   Quoted by Tony Barber in the *Independent* newspaper, March 21, 2003.

5   The information and story of Kada Hotic comes from an interview with her carried out by the author in May 2010, parts of which appeared in *Wired* magazine in August 2010, and from another interview carried out on behalf of the author in Sarajevo in 2013; other parts of the story come from numerous and multiple pieces of interview testimony and description given by her to the media, human rights groups, and judicial proceedings in her capacity, among other things, as a leading member of the Association of Mothers of Srebrenica and Žepa from 1995 to the present.

6   Quoted by Tim Ripley in *Operation Deliberate Force* (London: CDISS, 1999).

7   Interviews with the author, 2012.

8   Information about the operations around the fall of Srebrenica and its aftermath are drawn from quoted sources, but large parts of the account are derived from the indictment for genocide and other charges served against VRS General-Major Radislav Krstić of the Drina Corps of the Bosnian Serb Army by the ICTY, dated November 1, 1998, the judgment

prior to his sentencing to 46 years by the ICTY on charges of genocide on August 2, 2001, and the reduction of his sentence to 35 years on charges of aiding and abetting genocide by the ICTY Appeals Chamber on April 19, 2004. On this date the ICTY Appeals Chamber also upheld the judgment that genocide was committed at Srebrenica.

9   Transcript of cockpit HUD tapes and later interview with Lieutenant Manja Blok in Dutch media and on Fighter Ops website. Also quoted by Michael Dobbs on *Foreign Policy*'s website, and in *Check Point* magazine, May 2006.

10   Evidence in the trial of Radislav Krstić at the ICTY, April 2001.

11   Interview with the author, Sarajevo, May 2012.

12   Interviews with the author, 2006, 2012; interview with *Macleans*, Canada, July 14, 2005.

13   Testimony in the ICTY trial of Ratko Mladić, April 18, 2013.

14   Mladić's initial indictment by the ICTY, dated July 24 and November 4, 1995; the amended indictment of October 10, 2002; the first amended indictment of June 1, 2011; the second amended indictment of October 20, 2011; and the third amended indictment of December 16, 2011.

15   Number given by Bosnian Serb Army colonel Radislav Jankovic to Major Franken of the UN Dutch battalion, cited in the Netherlands Institute of War Documentation, 2002.

16   Although predominantly filled with Bosnian Muslims, the ranks of the ABiH contained Croats and Serbs too.

17   Verbatim testimony in the ICTY trial of Radislav Krstić.

18   Testimony in the Krstić trial and others.

19   Judgment of Radislav Krstić at the ICTY, August 2, 2001.

20   Ibid.

21   Ibid.

22   Ibid.

23   Major Dragan Obrenović was indicted by the ICTY on charges of war crimes and crimes against humanity in 2001.

24   ICTY judgment in the case of Dragan Jokić and Vidoje Blagojević, January 17, 2005.

25   Judgment in the trial of Radislav Krstić.

26   The trial of Dražen Erdemović began in The Hague on May 31, 1996, and on November 29, 1996, he was sentenced to ten years in prison. He testified several times in other trials.

27   Testimony in the trial of Radislav Krstić.

28   ICTY judgment in the case of Dragan Jokić and Vidoje Blagojević, January 17, 2005.

29   ICTY evidence documentation used in the trial of Radislav Krstić.

30   The ICTY's 339-page judgment of January 17, 2005, in the case of Vidoje Blagojević and Dragan Jokić, for instance, details the name of the officer from the Zvornik Brigade who was to sign one set of fuel requisitions.

31   Testimony and evidential material in the trial of Vidoje Blagojević and Dragan Jokić at the ICTY, January 17, 2005.

Chapter Three: How the Killers Tried to Hide the Evidence

1   Testimony of General Smith to the ICTY, trial of Momčilo Perišić, May 2009.

2   Interview by the author with UK defense analyst Professor Tim Ripley, 2013.

3   Opening statements by prosecutor Peter McCloskey in the trial of Ratko Mladić at the ICTY, May 16, 2011; ICTY indictment against Mladić.

4   ICTY mandate, ICTY website.

5   *US vs. Van Leeb,* 1948.

6   ICTY indictments and judgments in Srebrenica trials.

7   Testimony of protected witness P-135, as cited in the ICTY judgment of Vidoje Blagojević and Dragan Jokic, January 17, 2005.

8   Quoted by Marlise Simons in "Report says Serbs tormented 2 French Pilots," *New York Times,* December 29, 2005; and by Emma Daly in "NATO believes French pilots killed by Serbs," *Independent,* October 21, 1995. The French newspaper story was based upon a French government report and an interview with the father of one of the pilots.

9   Ed Vulliamy, *Observer,* 2006.

10   Interview with the author, Kosovo, June 1999.

Chapter Four: Digging up the Evidence of Mass Murder

1   Interviews with the author, June 2012 to February 2013.

2   Ian Hanson, interview with the author.

3   Interview with Meg Bortin of the *New York Times,* August 8, 2008.

4   Along with the ICTY, another totally separate international criminal tribunal had also been set up to deal with the 1994 Rwandan genocide. It was based in Arusha, Tanzania.

5   Interview with the author.

6   Interview with UK military ammunition technical officer, Royal Logistics Corps, Sarajevo, 2011.

7   Malcolm J. Dodd, *Terminal Ballistics—A Text and Atlas of Gunshot Wounds* (Boca Raton, Florida: CRC Press / Taylor & Francis, 2006).

8   See Chapter Five—the ICMP collected whole and fragmented clothing samples from the remains and surroundings of over 20,000 buried corpses or parts thereof in the Balkans alone.

9   Interviewee's personal blog; interview with the author, August 2012.

10   ICTY indictment of Milan Kovačević and Simo Drljača, filed on March 13, 1997.

Chapter Five: Inside Kosovo, Serbia, and the World of the Missing

1   The respective missing persons commissions from the Muslim-Croat Federation and the Republika Srpska.

2   International Rescue Committee.

3 ICTY website.

4 Along with representatives of the Associated Press, the author was one of the first journalists to arrive in the village after NATO troops entered Kosovo in June 1999. The group of journalists discovered the mass grave containing the Kosovo Albanian victims, and over a series of subsequent visits to the village, the author was shown the impromptu memorial to the murdered children.

5 The author, along with Maggie O'Kane from the British newspaper the *Guardian,* was one of the first journalists to arrive at the site of the killings in Suva Reka in June 1999.

6 Belgrade War Crimes Court proceedings.

7 Interview between Stankovic and Dan Bilevsky, "Bosnia fugitive is hero to some, butcher to others," *New York Times,* August 3, 2008.

8 The CIA admitted in a statement on July 22, 1999, that the Chinese Embassy had been hit by NATO, but that the strike was "unintended."

9 Meeting with the author, Bujumbura, 1996—the latter was at the time the Reuters correspondent for Burundi from December 1995 to June 10, 1996.

10 The words became the title of a film about the Bosnian war, *In the Land of Blood and Honey,* written and directed by Angelina Jolie and released in 2011.

Chapter Six: Building a Human Identification System

1 Interview with the author, Sarajevo, December 2012.

2 Interview with the author, May 2010.

3 Kosovo was formally a province of Serbia until February 2008, when it declared independence, which was widely recognized internationally. At the time of writing in March 2013, countries that had recognized this status included the United States, the United Kingdom, Australia, France, and Germany, as well as 51 percent of UN member states, 22 out of 27 EU countries, and 24 out of 28 NATO member states. Serbia has not recognized it.

4 The descriptions of the establishment of the ICMP's DNA laboratory system and the workings of DNA-assisted identification are based upon verbal, personal, and written interviews and written exchanges with ICMP staff of all levels and the author's personal experience of working with the organization from 2008–2010, of writing about it as a journalist between 2007–2012, and of attending briefings about its operations. ICMP standard operating procedure reports and documents provided some of the information. Background reading of extracts from such established texts as Robert Olby's *The Path to the Double Helix: The Discovery of DNA* (Seattle: University of Washington Press, 1974, rev. ed. 1994) helped. It should be stressed that any errors or factual inaccuracies in this area are the author's, and his alone.

Chapter Seven: The Wind of Change in Serbia

1   Interviews between the author and a former senior Western diplomat based in the former Yugoslavia between 1996 and 2002.
2   ICMP Case Resolution Analysis Report, November 26, 2008.
3   Interview with the author; the article quoted appeared in the *IHT* on July 7, 2000.
4   The author was at the scene of the bombing shortly after it happened and reported at the funeral.

Chapter Eight: The World of the Missing, Post-9/11

1   Estimates of the ICMP.
2   Reuters, April 16, 2001; Radio B-92 in Belgrade, April 16; ICTY.
3   Reuters, April 16, 2001.
4   Interview with the author, Sarajevo, October 2012.
5   Interview with the author, August 2012.
6   Interview with Beth Kampschror, "RS Prime Minister Attends Srebrenica anniversary ceremony," *Southeast European Times*, July 14, 2003.
7   Interview with the author.
8   Wesley Clark's testimony in court in closed session during the trial of Slobodan Milošević, December 15 and 16, 2003.
9   Interview with the BBC following Ratko Mladić's arrest, May 2011.

Chapter Nine: Global Operations Begin

1   The author accompanied and facilitated Professor Inge Morild's visit to the ICMP.
2   See www.feldgrau.com; nuav.net; Sven Goll, "Death in an Arctic Bog," *Aftenposten*, August 5, 2008; Alan Hall, *Scotsman*, August 7, 2008; and Alfred Steurich, *Gebirgsjäger im Bild: 6.SS-Gebirgsdivision Nord 1940–1945*, (Germany: Munin Verlag).
3   Kaprolat Committee.
4   Thomas Parsons et al., "Success Rates of Nuclear Short Tandem Repeat Typing from Different Skeletal Elements," *Croatian Medical Journal* 48 (2007): 486–93.
5   Interpol Secretary General's acceptance speech, Berlin, September 2005.
6   Cebu City and Manila media, August–September 2008.
7   Statement by the ICMP director-general, June 16, 2008.
8   The author was with her when she signed the agreement.
9   In February 1991, the Chilean National Commission for Truth and Reconciliation released its report encompassing human rights abuses resulting in death or disappearance committed in Chile during the years of military rule under Augusto Pinochet (1973–1990). According to the report, 2,296 people were murdered during the seventeen-year period.

10   The law, largely drafted and designed by the ICMP, was designed to protect and ensure the economic and social rights of those who had missing
relatives, and was adopted by the parliament of Bosnia and Herzegovina
in 2004. Its subsequent implementation was to be haphazard.

Chapter Ten: Rule of Law, Not Rule of War

1   ICMP Tracking Chart for the Former Yugoslavia, July 30, 2010.

2   ICMP press release, November 6, 2009.

3   This quote was provided to the author for use in the promotion of the
book but originated in a quote made by Professor Morling on March 26,
2010, about the ICMP.

4   The ICTY announced on December 12, 2012, that Zdravko Tolimir,
former assistant commander and chief for intelligence and security of
the main staff of the Bosnian Serb Army (VRS), was sentenced to life
imprisonment.

5   Iraq body count.

6   Interview with the author, May 2012.

7   Interviews, conversations, reports, and documentation from assorted family associations of missing persons in Bosnia, Serbia, Kosovo, and Croatia
read, carried out, and documented by the author, 1999–2012.

8   Interview with the author, May 2010.

9   Aida Cerkez-Robinson, "How many times can you bury your child before
you go mad?" Associated Press, July 2009.

Chapter Eleven: Ratko Mladić's Last Request

1   Different interviews, reports, and statements, including interview with the
BBC and Nenad Popovic; Serbian interior ministry and presidential statement; media interviews with neighbors; Serbian MUP sources; Belgrade
War Crimes Prosecutor; and Office of the President et al., on May 26, 27,
and 28, 2011.

2   See Julian Borger, *Guardian*, April 2, 2013, for one account.

3   *Economist*, May 27, 2012.

4   Queen's, or King's, Counsel is a status awarded to successful, experienced
barristers and advocates by the Crown of England that is recognized by
courts.

5   The official title is "The Extraordinary Chambers in the Courts of
Cambodia."

6   Jackson's opening statement is published in *Trials of the Major War
Criminals Before the International Military Tribunal 98–155* (Nuremberg:
IMT, 1947), a collection known sometimes as "the Blue Set," and in his
own book *The Nürnberg Case* (New York: Alfred A. Knopf, 1947; rpt New
York: Cooper Square Publishers, 1971), and it is available on the web, as
part of the full record of the proceedings before the IMT, through the

Avalon Project at Yale Law School and from the website of the Robert H. Jackson Center.

7   Interview with the author by e-mail from Cambodia, July 2012 and February 2013.

8   BIRN, "Spotlight on Mladić: Villain or Celebrity? The Arrest and Trial of Ratko Mladić in the Balkan Media," Sarajevo, 2012.

9   *Dnevni Avaz,* June 4, 2011, as quoted in the above BIRN publication.

10   Ibid.

11   Quoted in *Slobodna Bosna,* May 27, 2011.

12   All three are quoted in the BIRN report.

13   Ibid.

14   Interviews with the author, May 2012, December 2012, and January 2013.

15   Testimony, prosecution opening statements, and proceedings in the opening of the trial of Ratko Mladić at the ICTY in The Hague on May 15, 16, and 17, 2011.

16   Ibid.

17   Testimony of former general Sir Rupert Smith in the trial of Ratko Mladić at the ICTY, January 2013.

18   Judgment against Vidoje Blagojević and Dragan Jokić at the ICTY, January 17, 2005.

19   Judgment at the ICTY in the trial of Popovic et al., June 10, 2010.

20   Testimony of former OTP investigator Dusan Janc at the ICTY in the trial of Zdravko Tolimir, May 14, 2010.

21   Interview by the author with the legal and policy director of the ICMP, January 2013.

22   Ibid.

23   Ibid.

24   Interviews with the author in person and by e-mail, November 2012 and January 2013.

25   Ibid.

26   Interviews with the author in person and by e-mail, November 2012–March 2013.

Chapter Twelve: From Srebrenica to Kurdistan, Brazzaville, and Libya

1   Interview with the author by e-mail from Erbil, Kurdistan, December 2012.

2   Quote given by him on a visit to Bosnia, May 2012.

3   ICMP press release, November 12, 2012.

4   Interview with the author, November 2012.

Index